Thames & Hudson

ON THE HIGH LINE

By ANNIK LA FARGE

Preface, additional text, and photographs
RICK DARKE

Principal photography
SCOTT MLYN
JUAN VALENTIN

Art direction and design
LORRAINE FERGUSON

CONTENTS

GANSEVOORT— 14TH STREETS

14TH–16TH STREETS

16TH–20TH STREETS

INTRODUCTION

by Annik La Farge

In the years since the old railroad trestle known as the High Line first opened to the public in 2009 it has been heralded for many things: its beautiful gardens, and landscape and architectural design; the singular views it offers of New York City from thirty feet above the street; its multimedia art installations and cultural programs; and the coming together of community leaders and city government to create a remarkable public place that embodies new ideas about modern urban landscape design and sustainability.

But there's another aspect of the High Line that makes a visit here richly rewarding. The High Line tells a story, and walking the length of this 1.45-mile park provides a unique way to experience the many-layered narrative that makes up New York's colorful history.

When it opened for business in 1934, the elevated railroad was referred to as "the lifeline of New York" because it was an essential artery for the delivery of dairy, meat, and produce from all over the country. But the neighborhood that the former railroad traverses, from Gansevoort to 34th Street, has been a vital center of commerce and industry for more than a century. First there were outdoor markets, then factories and warehouses. Today, giant Internet, software, media, and fashion companies flourish alongside art galleries, restaurants, and boutiques. Cutting through, and above, the old neighborhood is the new "park in the sky."

To fully understand the historical roots of the High Line one needs first to look a bit west to New York's other lifeline, the Hudson River, whose deepwater harbor with its extraordinarily rich diversity of fish, plant, and animal life was the original attraction of Manhattan Island, first to Native Americans, then to Europeans. Described by one writer as "a thread that runs through the fabric of four centuries of American history," the Hudson has played a central role in the narrative of the United States since the Dutch established New Amsterdam in the 17th century. It was vital to George Washington's military strategy; nearly one-third of the battles of the Revolutionary War took place on or near its banks. The Hudson soon became the young country's most vital transportation thoroughfare, enabling packet lines, clipper ships, and steamboats to transport all manner of goods, from beaver pelts and food supplies to building products. The fruits of commerce came to New York Harbor from around the world, traveled up the Hudson to the Erie Canal, which opened in 1825, then west to a developing nation.

And then came the railroads.

The story of the High Line has its true beginnings in February 1832, when construction began on the first railroad in New York: the New York and Harlem Railroad. In those days railcars were pulled by horses and could attain a speed of seven miles per hour. The railroads rapidly expanded, and in 1846 the City of New York authorized the laying of tracks along a thirteen-mile corridor beginning at Canal Street and running up Tenth, Eleventh, and Twelfth Avenues to Spuyten Duyvil in the Bronx. In the 1850s, Commodore Cornelius Vanderbilt, then the richest man in America, sold off his shipping interests and began to acquire railroads; in 1868, on parkland formerly owned by Trinity Church, Vanderbilt erected a massive stone depot to receive the trains of his New York Central line. He named it St. John's Park Terminal, after a church that had been torn down to accommodate his growing empire. And lest anyone forget who was king of the railroad, the Commodore placed a

RMS Queen Mary arriving in the New York Harbor, early 1900s. Courtesy New York State Archives, Education Department, Division of Visual Instruction, Instructional Lantern Slides, circa 1856–1939, A3045-78, Dn NY14.

Farmer's Market at Gansevoort Street, circa 1910s. Courtesy of the Irma and Paul Milstein Division of United States History, Local History and Genealogy, The New York Public Library, Stephen A. Schwarzman Building.

The West Side Cowboy, 1911. Photo George Grantham Bain.

towering bronze statue of himself on its roof.

During the second half of the 19th century and throughout the Industrial Revolution the trains of Vanderbilt's railroad passed through an area of lower Manhattan that was filled with factories large and small. There were ironworks and lumberyards, grain elevators and lard refineries, stockyards, abattoirs, candle factories, and manufacturers of everything from cigars to pianos. New businesses sprang up everywhere, from innovators like Western Electric, which enabled shippers to better communicate with each other, and the Manhattan Refrigerating Company, which developed the first system of industrial cold storage, to paper and box companies that made cartons for all the goods being transported.

As period photographs show, the lower west side of Manhattan was a vibrant, bustling chaos of merchants, grocers, stevedores, and horse-drawn carriages. The city must have known it would be dangerous to have so many trains running at grade through the streets of downtown, because it had passed an ordinance in the 1850s that required the railroad to "employ a proper person to precede the trains on horseback, to give the necessary warning in a suitable manner on their approach." The proper persons came to be known as "West Side Cowboys," and they waved a red flag by day and a red lantern by night to give their necessary warning. Still, so many pedestrians were injured or killed by trains that Tenth Avenue came to be known as "Death Avenue."

It was in the 1920s that plans were made to elevate the freight tracks and remove the danger from the streets. But instead of running up the avenue as the old passenger trains — "the El's" — had done in previous years, the High Line would cut through the middle of the block. Companies with foresight, like R. C. Williams wholesale grocer, saw an opportunity: they constructed warehouses and factories along the new rail line and installed loading docks that opened out onto the tracks. Train engineers simply pulled their locomotives up alongside the buildings, cargo was transferred, and the trains continued on their way. A separate spur was created at 16th Street to accommodate the National Biscuit Company; it allowed dairy trains from the nation's heartland to veer off the main tracks and unload milk and eggs, which the bakery's huge ovens would faithfully transform into Fig Newtons, Mallomars, Animal Crackers, and more. Not only were lives saved by removing locomotives from the city's streets, but trucks no longer had to stand idle or get stuck in traffic on their way to and from the rail terminals.

Vanderbilt's depot was torn down in 1927 to make way for the entrance to the Holland Tunnel, which ushered in the next wave of modern freight transportation: trucks and tractor-trailers. A new terminal — called St. John's Freight Terminal — was built on Spring Street to accommodate the brand new High Line. The sprawling structure occupied three full city blocks and more closely connected the elevated railroad to the hub of maritime commerce at the Hudson River piers, just 150 yards to the west. Trains traveling south on the High Line entered the second floor of the terminal from one of eight feeder tracks; once inside, fourteen freight elevators were available to transport goods to the ground floor, where as many as 150 trucks could simultaneously load or unload cargo. The structure even included two refrigerated rooms for the storage of perishable freight.

For forty-six years, beginning in 1934, trains ran along the elevated tracks of the High Line by day and by night, cutting through buildings, rumbling below tenement windows, speeding the delivery of countless products to their ultimate destinations around the country and the globe. But with the rise of interstate trucking, global air travel, and containerized shipping, the mighty railroads began to fade, and in 1980 the last train ran on the High Line, pulling three boxcars reputedly filled with Thanksgiving turkeys. St. John's ceased operating as a rail terminal in the 1960s, and the High Line south of Gansevoort Street was torn down in stages; the final piece, connecting Gansevoort and Bank Streets, was removed in 1991.

* * *

The second half of the High Line's story begins in August 1999 when two young men attended a community planning board meeting about the future of the defunct railroad. Joshua David and Robert Hammond didn't know each other before that meeting, but something about the structure and its history galvanized them and led to the founding of Friends of the High Line. A classic urban battle ensued, pitting the Davids of preservation against the Goliaths of city bureaucracy. For

ten years the nonprofit group led the fight to save the High Line, arguing against those who considered it an eyesore and — worse — an obstruction to the ancient fine art of real estate development. The group raised money, gained support from celebrities and politicians, studied modern urban landscape design, and became expert in navigating the treacherous labyrinth of New York City politics. Meanwhile, the old viaduct went to seed.

In the years following the railroad's demise the sturdy but rusting railbed had transformed into what some have called "a meadow in the sky." Here, in the middle of Manhattan, running through the Meatpacking District and West Chelsea, was a wild garden filled with roses, ailanthus trees, dandelions, Virginia creeper, black cherry, chives, and acres of the incomparably elegant Queen Anne's lace, bending in the breeze just thirty tantalizing feet above oblivious city traffic.

When Robert Hammond brought landscape photographer Joel Sternfeld to the abandoned railroad on a cold March day in 2000 to take pictures for the group's fundraising effort, the sight took Sternfeld's breath away. *Give me a year*, the photographer pleaded. And so they did. As it turned out the photographs Sternfeld took would fuel the vision of the entire preservation project. The resulting landscape — designed by Field Operations with Diller Scofidio + Renfro, winners of an international design competition, and plant design by the brilliant Dutch horticulturist Piet Oudolf — in many ways seeks to pay tribute to what Sternfeld captured in his photographs and early visitors to the derelict railroad had found so magical. Unlike Central Park, which Frederick Law Olmsted conceived in the 1850s (when the first rail tracks were being laid in lower Manhattan) as "a surrogate Adirondack landscape where ordinary people could get away from their urban surroundings," the High Line was designed not as an antidote to the city but as a platform that puts the great metropolis on glorious display: its beauties as well as its blights. The park cuts through the city, *is part of* the city, and therefore allows us to see and experience it in an entirely new way, from a perspective never enjoyed before.

The project became a huge success, attracting millions of visitors a year, and has inspired cities around the country and the world to preserve the infrastructure of a long-gone industrial era and

The High Line at dusk, looking north from 17th Street.

transform it into idyllic public spaces. Beauty in decay, resurrected in new form.

* * *

On the High Line was designed to capture the spirit and beauty of this remarkable place and to answer the many questions a visitor might have about the mile-and-a-half-long steel trestle, the design of the park itself, the surrounding architecture, and the industries that thrived in its neighborhoods across the centuries. It's not a narrative with a beginning, middle, and end, but it does follow a rough linear path from Gansevoort Street, the park's southern entrance, to 30th Street. Like the High Line itself, which has nine points of entry, the reader can open the book at any page and get a piece of the story and a view of the park. Or it can be read through, from start to finish, south to north. Along the way, the text aims to serve as an ideal, educated travel companion, someone invisibly perched on your shoulder who periodically whispers in your ear:

See that pier over there, number 54? That's where, in 1912, the **Carpathia** delivered survivors of the **Titanic**, which had been heading for Pier 59, now the driving range at the Chelsea Piers.

Or: *Check out those rusting metal meat hooks near the Standard Hotel. That's how animal carcasses were transferred from freight train to meatpacking plant.*

And: *That large yellow flower that's tilting over the railing? It's a compass plant. Its flower follows the course of the sun; early American pioneers used it like a compass to identify which direction was west or east.*

The story of the High Line is, of course, not quite finished. The final section of the park, which wraps around the West Side Rail Yards and extends to 34th Street, remains a wild garden. In late 2011 CSX, the railroad behemoth that ultimately absorbed Commodore Vanderbilt's New York Central and countless other railroads that went bankrupt during the 20th century, agreed to donate the remaining part of the structure to the city. Major donations were announced and Friends of the High Line was well on its way in the fundraising effort for section three.

So more change is coming, but this is the inevitable end to any story that involves New York City. As long ago as 1856 a writer for *Harper's Monthly* lamented that New York "is never the same city for a dozen years together. A man born in New York forty years ago finds nothing, absolutely nothing, of the New York he knew." Change comes faster nowadays, and a visitor to today's High Line will find a quite different park when he returns in just a few years. This is both by design and by accident. Piet Oudolf deliberately selected plants that would present an ever-changing and always intriguing landscape throughout the course of the year, from the height of the summer season to the cold, windy days of winter. And already one can see results of the decisions that the gardening staff is making about which plants or grasses might dominate in one place and which might prevail in another. Meanwhile, all along the High Line, on both sides of the structure, new buildings are popping up — as many as forty, by one count, went up in the first two years that the park was open. As the success of the High Line spurs development in the neighborhood, the feel of open space, the presence of light, the play of shadows, and even the sounds of the city itself are transforming and evolving.

This is, perhaps, the enduring theme of the High Line's story. If you stand at the northern end of the park and close your eyes as the captain of a giant cruise line sounds the bellowing horn of his ship, you can almost imagine what an early-20th-century visitor saw from the streets below as the breathtakingly elegant ocean liners — the *Queen Mary*, the *Normandie*, the *Ile de France* — sailed into New York Harbor when it was the largest, most important port in the world. The High Line, this quintessentially modern, linear park, connects us to our past while embracing every vista of our present. In the pages that follow we'll help you see how it all came to be as you take your walk through New York's new garden in the sky.

PREFACE

by Rick Darke

I aimed my camera at the High Line as it angled southeast from the 30th Street Yards, and the letters "PARK" filled the viewfinder. I took this as an omen. It was late January 2003. I was photographing in the cold rain and snow, and the lettering on the trestle's blackened steel actually read "PARKING." A smokestack echoed the distant spire of the Empire State Building while, glistening in the wetness, razor wire stretched over every possible entry point from where I was standing south to Gansevoort Street to discourage casual visitors from a walk on the Line. It was all a bit forbidding — and beautiful.

A New York Central Lines Alco RS-3 diesel locomotive rides the rails near the 30th Street yards in Jim Shaughnessy's 1957 photo.

The same section of the High Line is disused and hung with razor wire in this 2003 photo.

Like the weathered ghost of a New York Central Lines logo surviving nearby on the trestle, the parking sign dated to a time when powerful locomotives thrummed overhead, essential to the city's West Side commerce, to an era in which railroads were paramount, America's strength was made of steel, and the spectacular promise of

American machines and heavy industry was defining a new aesthetic. Called Machine Age Modern, Industrial Modern, or sometimes Depression Modern, it has generally aged well for the good reason that the best examples are utterly unpretentious. There is no better example of no-nonsense form following function than the steel-plated face

October 2002, the surreal beauty of the unreconstructed High Line is apparent.

"PARKING" is still legible on a wet winter day in 2003.

Rivets, rust, and ghost of a New York Central Lines logo in 2003.

A mural bids urban explorers in 2003 to "Save the Tracks."

of the High Line. Every rivet and every pattern in the plates contributes to the strength of the structure. The decorative railings visible wherever the trestle crosses a street are brilliantly crafted of the same heavy-gauge steel, the design so durably elegant it has become an indelible symbol of the High Line park.

I'd first walked the elevated tracks in 2002 when invited by Friends of the High Line cofounders Robert Hammond and Joshua David to join a small group of professionals, all escorted for security purposes by a representative of CSX, the railroad that owned and was liable for the Line. As a botanist and photographer who had for decades been focused on the ecology of transportation corridors, I was familiar with the unusual perspectives and compelling vistas often afforded by such places, but I was unprepared for what I saw on the High Line. It was at once exhilarating and disorienting. I'd known the city since childhood, yet I'd never witnessed anything remotely like these apparently infinite vistas with not a single automobile in sight. It was like strolling through Hugh Ferriss's imaginary *Metropolis of Tomorrow*, in which pedestrians were safely elevated above speeding traffic on dedicated walkways spanning even the broadest avenues. It was exhilarating because for once I could pay attention to the city itself — its shapes and forms, sounds and colors — without worrying about stepping into the path of an oncoming vehicle. It was disorienting because of the immense scale and extreme clarity of the expanses, undiminished by windows or windshields, entirely exposed to the elements.

Hugh Ferriss's charcoal rendering of architect Harvey Wiley Corbett's "Proposal to Increase Street Capacity," from the *Regional Plan of New York and Its Environs* (1923–24).

In his 1998 book, *Outside Lies Magic,* John Stilgoe writes of the wonders apparent to any outdoor explorer willing to seek the extraordinary in the ordinary, and suggests: "Outside lies unprogrammed awareness that at times becomes directed serendipity." He could easily have been describing a walk on the High Line any time after the trains stopped running. Joel Sternfeld's early photographs of the High Line in its wild state continue to resonate with anyone yearning for a bit of open space removed from the relentless scripting of modern urban life. The High Line was, and still is, a perfect place to practice the art of observation. It is rich with intrigue because it is full of chance. Myriad processes responsible for building the Line, abandoning the Line, and then filling it with life are still at work, making each day, each season, each year different than the next.

One of the common questions raised by visitors is *What grew on the High Line before it became a park, and how much of it was native?* The short answer is that the spontaneous vegetation inhabiting the interstices between the tracks was a mix of species from North America, Europe, and Asia. Some were beautiful, some not, but all were adapted to conditions on the site, which by gardening standards were extremely challenging. The "soil" supporting these wildlings was decomposed organic matter that had accumulated in the spaces between the coarse gravel ballast. Available moisture was only what fell from the sky, augmented by condensation. The High Line, past and present, is essentially one big green roof. Rooting depth is often only a foot or less. Like any bridge, it freezes faster, and unless irrigated the sun and reflected heat make for sizzling summer conditions. Despite this, over 160 plant species were thriving on the High Line by 2003, when Richard Stalter submitted his report "The Flora on the High Line, New York City, New York" to the Torrey Botanical Society. How much of this was native? According to Stalter, 82 species were native and 79 were introduced exotics. The natives were the majority — they were "winning"; but by most measures a score of 82–79 is nothing for either team to feel badly about. I'm deeply ambivalent about keeping score based on origin when the real game is about adaptability and ecological function. Queen Anne's lace (*left*), for example, is a commonly beautiful component of the still-wild West Side Rail Yards section. A rela-

tive of the cultivated carrot that has been used medicinally by humans for millennia, this Eurasian species was introduced to North America by humans hundreds of years ago. It creates oxygen, sequesters carbon, and provides shelter and sustenance for a mix of native and introduced insects. And it thrives thirty feet in the air in the middle of the city. I'm ready to accord it honorary native status, but then exactly how does anyone define a native New Yorker?

This late April 2003 photo illustrates the plainly unremarkable vegetation then present at many points along the Line.

A preliminary excavation in 2005 reveals the shallow depth of available rooting space between the tracks and the concrete liner of the High Line's steel trestle.

Overleaf: The view north in May 2005 as the High Line crosses West 22nd Street. Pigeons perched on rooftop railings have a view of tree of heaven seedlings growing in the stone ballast. Graffiti competes with original signage lingering on the brick above the former loading dock of Spear & Company's bonded warehouse (at left).

Another common question about the High Line is, *Couldn't the existing wild gardens have been saved when making the new park?* To this the short answer is *Probably not, and maybe yet.* "Probably not" because for considerable stretches the spontaneous vegetation consisted mostly of insignificant annual and perennial species that have little presence except at the height of the growing season. Few visitors would have viewed these as anything but weeds, and great lengths of the park would have appeared somewhat desolate for two or three seasons each year. "Maybe yet" because the High Line's most visually compelling wild gardens have always been located at the West Side Rail Yards, and these remain largely intact. The readily accessible beauty here owes much to the setting. This is where carpets of luminous low grasses glow in the morning and evening sun, punctuated by shrubs and sweeps of wildflowers. The grasses' soft texture highlights the curving patterns of the rails, and the entire landscape is accompanied by unsurpassed views of the Hudson River. Though the future of this section is uncertain, since Friends of the High Line has succeeded in securing rights to it, there is a real chance the rail yards' wild gardens will play an authentic role in the park's final section.

In 2004, responding to the design proposals of four finalist teams competing for the opportunity to create a master plan for the project, FHL cofounder Robert Hammond suggested the High Line would become "this generation's Central Park." Certainly Central Park has no equal in New York City, so what's uniquely generational about the High Line? It's all in the cultural context. Central Park was designed as a countrified retreat from unhealthy urban conditions directly or indirectly attributable to the Industrial Revolution, which was then looming ever larger. Although Central Park is completely artificial in that its landscapes were entirely designed, its inspiration was an idyllic Nature, rural in form and content. In contrast, the High Line is inspired by a Nature comprised of a motley crew of global souls — a literal melting pot of eminently urban species adapted to postindustrial landscapes. The Industrial Revolution in America is now part of a misty past, and though machinery is more pervasive than ever, it is less palpable, increasingly residing in the Cloud. Today's generation is entertained by a profoundly evolved viewpoint, and the High Line represents this like no place before. It is a revolutionary landscape, romantically postindustrial and progressive in its embrace of emerging ecologies. It strikes a brilliant balance between gritty and pretty. A walk on the High Line provides an unequalled opportunity to reflect on New York City past, present, and future, out of doors in the nuanced Nature of our time.

Say what some poets will, Nature is not so much her own ever-sweet interpreter, as the mere supplier of that cunning alphabet, whereby selecting and combining as he pleases, each man reads his own peculiar lesson according to his own peculiar mind and mood.

— Herman Melville
Pierre, or the Ambiguities, 1852

Overleaf: Steel rails provide the landscape's organizing motif as they run through a spontaneous garden of low grasses, chives, and dwarf bearded iris at the West Side Rail Yards in May 2005.

Readers of poetry see the factory-village and the railway,
and fancy that the poetry of the landscape is broken up by these . . .
the poet sees them fall within the great Order
not less than the beehive or the spider's geometrical web.

— Ralph Waldo Emerson
From "The Poet," first published in *Essays: Second Series*, 1844

ON THE HIGH LINE

GANSEVOORT–14TH STREETS

14TH–16TH STREETS

16TH–20TH STREETS

20TH–23RD STREETS

23RD–26TH STREETS

26TH–30TH STREETS

30TH–34TH STREETS

Mountain mint, *Pychantus* ... et in mid-August.

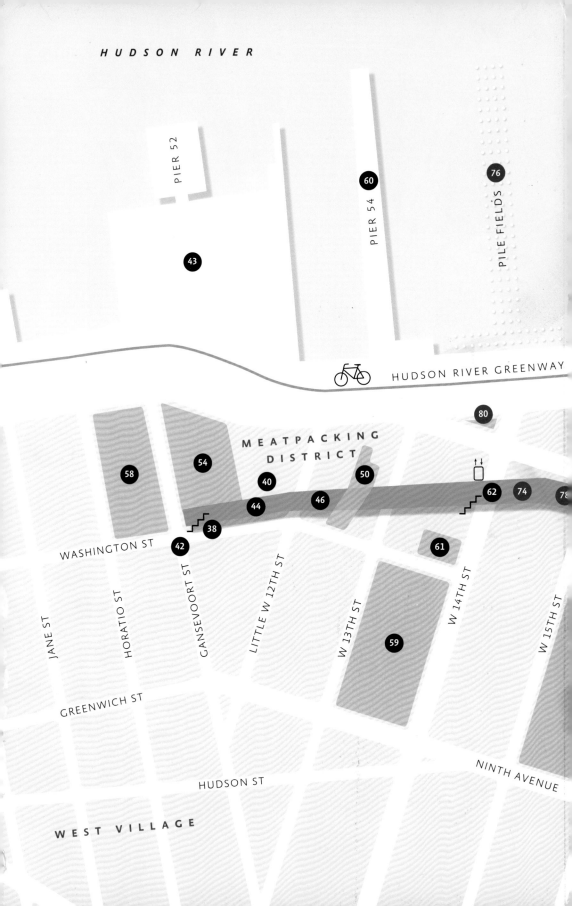

HUDSON RIVER

PIER 52

PIER 54

60

76

PILE FIELDS

43

HUDSON RIVER GREENWAY

80

MEATPACKING
DISTRICT

58

54

40

50

62

74

78

44

46

38

42

61

WASHINGTON ST

JANE ST

HORATIO ST

GANSEVOORT ST

LITTLE W 12TH ST

W 13TH ST

59

W 14TH ST

W 15TH ST

GREENWICH ST

HUDSON ST

NINTH AVENUE

WEST VILLAGE

Yellow onion, *Allium obliquum*, and red clover, *Trifolium rubens*, brighten the High Line's early June landscape near the Tenth Avenue Square.

PIER 57

77

113 CHELSEA PIERS

ELEVENTH AVENUE

126

126

87

122

142

86

84

88

102

124

90

91

98

136

108

145

144

144

W 16TH ST

W 17TH ST

W 18TH ST

W 19TH ST

TENTH AVENUE

W 20TH ST

W 21ST ST

127

TWELFTH AVENUE

WEST CHELSEA

ELEVENTH AVENUE

CHELSEA

W 22ND ST

W 23RD ST

W 24TH ST

W 25TH ST

W 26TH ST

W 27TH ST

W 28TH ST

143

147

148

146

151

162

165

164

171

186

155

173

190

182

183

199

Stonecrop, *Sedum telephium* 'Matrona', thrives in full sun and dry, sharply drained conditions such as those found in the coarse gravel between the High Line's pavers at 17th Street.

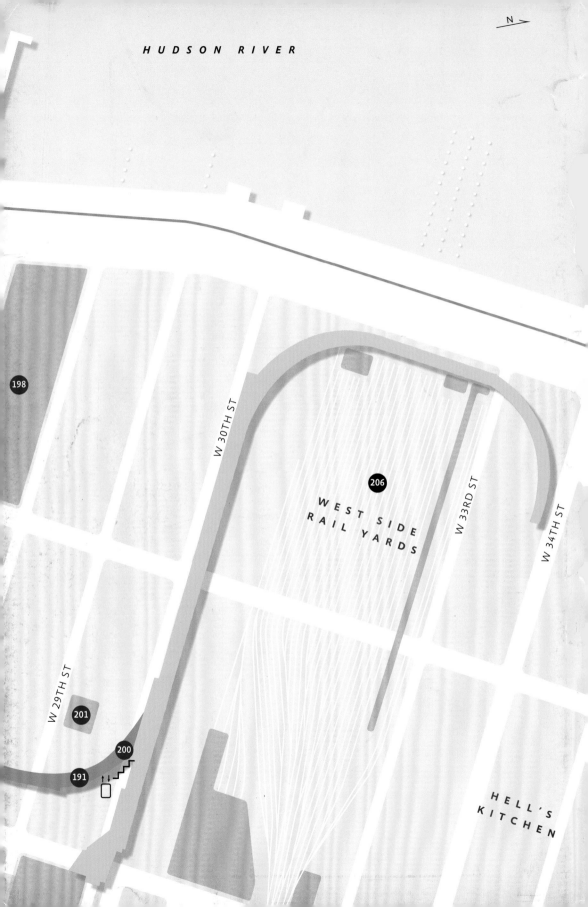

HUDSON RIVER

198

W 30TH ST

WEST SIDE
RAIL YARDS

206

W 33RD ST

W 34TH ST

W 29TH ST

201

200

191

HELL'S
KITCHEN

Steel rails thread through an autumn mosaic of alumroot, asters, goldenrods, and grasses on the Northern Spur.

ON THE HIGH LINE

Cartography by Marty Schnure

MANHATTAN

High
Line

202 — 30th–34th Streets

184 — 26th–30th Streets

158 — 23rd–26th Streets

132 — 20th–23rd Streets

96 — 16th–20th Streets

72 — 14th–16th Streets

36 — Gansevoort–14th Streets

Stair entrance

Elevator access

Public restroom

Bike path

98   Page reference

Length of High Line: 1.45 miles

GANSEVOORT–14TH STREETS

THE SLOW STAIRS

To create the grand entrance at Gansevoort Street construction crews cut through the steel beams of the former elevated railroad, taking care to preserve as much of the original structure as possible. These are the "slow stairs" of the High Line: a long ascent of forty-five steps that encourages a visitor to contemplate the sturdy industrial infrastructure that supports a space of remarkable elegance and beauty above street level.

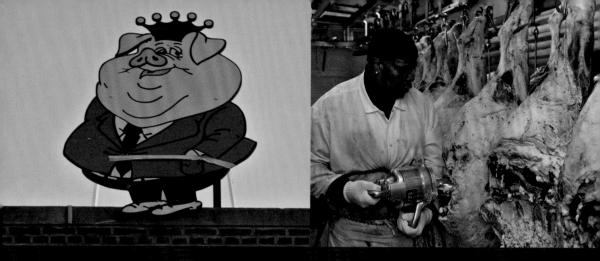

THE MEATPACKING DISTRICT

The southern end of the High Line traverses one of New York's oldest and most historically significant neighborhoods, known today as the Meatpacking District. Since the 1840s it has been a vibrant center of industry and commerce, particularly for the food business. As early as 1879 there were outdoor farmers' markets here; the neighborhood filled with merchants who sold poultry, meat, seafood, eggs, butter, beer, liquor, and more. It also included some of the earliest and most technologically advanced cold-storage facilities, developed at the turn of the century by the Manhattan Refrigerating Company (*p.58*). This innovation, along with the

thriving port along Gansevoort Piers, enabled the district to become a key supplier to restaurants and hotels all over the city. There are still a handful of active businesses in the Meatpacking District, down from some 250 slaughterhouses and packing companies at the turn of the century. A dozen firms — some of which are third-generation, family-run businesses — operate from a city-owned building just under the High Line on land that was first owned and developed by the Astor family in the early 19th century. Today the meatpackers share the neighborhood with nightclubs, fashion designers, restaurants, and quintessentially 21st-century retailers like the Apple Store.

West Washington Street Market, New York City, early 1900s. New York State Archives, Education Department, Division of Visual Instruction, Instructional lantern slides, c. 1856–1939.

Activities begin at 4 a.m. Farmers in overalls and mud-caked shoes stand in trucks, shouting their wares. Commission merchants, pushcart vendors, and restaurant buyers trudge warily from one stand to another, digging arms into baskets of fruits or vegetables to ascertain quality. Trucks move continually in and out among the piled crates of tomatoes, beans, cabbages, lettuce, and other greens in the street. Hungry derelicts wander about in the hope of picking up a stray vegetable dropped from some truck while patient nuns wait to receive leftover, unsalable goods for distribution among the destitute.

— *The WPA Guide to New York City,* **1939**

Gansevoort–14th Streets

GANSEVOORT STREET

The very heart of the Meatpacking District is Gansevoort Street. The writer Michael Cunningham called it "a dark and melancholy beauty . . . probably the only street in Manhattan, and maybe in the world, where you could procure, in one easy trip, a side of beef and a 1970s sectional sofa in pristine condition." Herman Melville spent nineteen years as a customs-house inspector at the Gansevoort Dock, named after his maternal grandfather, Peter Gansevoort, a hero of the Battle of Saratoga. Melville worked on his last novel, *Billy Budd,* during these years.

THIRTEENTH AVENUE AND PIER 52

You won't find Thirteenth Avenue on any New York City map, but the southernmost end of the High Line affords one of the best views of the tiny portion that remains. Though it bears the rather pretentious name "Gansevoort Peninsula," it's a stubby little pier that's packed with garbage trucks and circled overhead by seagulls. Thirteenth Avenue has a tortured history; it was built on landfill that had been leased in the 1830s to businesses that wanted a foothold on the bustling waterfront, and extended from 11th to 29th Streets. But in the early 20th century the city realized there were greater fortunes to be made from the huge 800-foot luxury liners that were carrying thousands of visitors across the Atlantic Ocean each year. The federal government, which controls Manhattan's shoreline, wouldn't allow the city to extend the piers further into the Hudson River, so the city revoked the old leases and removed the landfill, thereby creating more shoreline on which to build the large, long structures of the Chelsea Piers.

Thirteenth Avenue was never a romantic place. In 1883 a reporter for the *New York Times* called it "a very peculiar avenue," a dirty footpath that ran through endless piles of lumber, past ice barges, schooners with mountains of coal on their decks, iron works, beer saloons, and lazy workers "who sit on timbers and lean up against things for hours at a time, silently sunning themselves, no doubt erroneously thinking that they think." Over the years spectacular fires destroyed dozens of buildings along Thirteenth Avenue: a candle factory, a grain elevator, a lard refinery, the Empire Print Works, a cotton warehouse.

Today Pier 52 consists of a salt shed and garage operated by the Department of Sanitation. It once had a large garbage incinerator on site, which was most famously used in 1956 by the Food and Drug Administration to burn more than six tons of books and articles by Wilhelm Reich. Once a respected colleague of Sigmund Freud, Reich became controversial after claiming to discover orgone, an essential "primordial cosmic energy" that could cure many ailments including cancer. He invented the "orgone energy accumulator," a large box in which his patients would sit — in the nude — and be exposed to the energy force. The FDA charged Reich with interstate traffic of an unsanctioned medical device and, after burning his life's work on the Gansevoort Peninsula, sent him to prison, where he died of heart failure.

Gansevoort Woodland

The area at the southern end of the park is known as the Gansevoort Woodland, a peaceful grove of gray birch, *Betula populifolia*. Often a pioneer species in fields and along abandoned railroads, the gray birch is rarely planted in formal gardens but is commonly found in woods and old industrial sites. It blooms in spring but is beautiful all year long, particularly at dusk when the clusters of trees are lit by warm spotlights that capture the distinctive pattern and texture of the bark. The High Line is bookended by this tree; a second grove of gray birch can be found at the northern end of the park, at 30th Street.

WASHINGTON GRASSLANDS

Just north of the Gansevoort Woodland is a garden that's markedly different from the sheltered grove: the Washington Grasslands, an open, often windy plaza of grasses, perennials, and shrubs. The former *New York Times* architecture critic Nicolai Ourossoff observed that the High Line "is conceived as a series of interwoven events, like chapters of a book." Looked at another way, this park, which runs through the largest art gallery district in the world, is a like a giant outdoor museum with different galleries or spaces filled with dozens of things to look at and appreciate. Those that were planned — the gardens and plants, architectural features, and lighting design — coexist alongside a helter-skelter of elements from the original cityscape: abandoned buildings with shattered windows, whorls and streaks of graffiti, rusted scaffolding, and an infinity of details from the neighborhood's manufacturing past.

Smokebush, *Cotinus* 'Grace'

Purple coneflower, *Echinacea purpurea*

Red switchgrass, *Panicum virgatum* 'Shenandoah'

SMOKEBUSH, TOADLILY, AND FRIENDS

The Washington Grasslands is a wide, open plaza that makes a perfect stage for the dramatic smokebush. "Kind of Dr. Seuss-y" is how one High Line gardener described *Cotinus* 'Grace,' an expansive and unwieldy tree whose leaves get darker — smokier — as the summer progresses and acquire a deep, purplish color in fall.

Visit the High Line in the fall and you might catch the toadlily, *Tricyrtis* 'Sinonome.' As National Public Radio contributor Ketzel Levine describes

this flower: "Its style (as in a plant's sexual parts) looks like a giraffe's neck, its anthers look like the eyes on a slug, its stamens arch like showerheads, and its six differently shaded petals (actually tepals) alternate like men and women at a dinner table. This whole surrealistic fantasy stands on three pairs of green rubber boots (swollen spurs that are part of the petals), which, kicked three times, reveal the source of the plant's Latin name: *tri*, meaning 'three,' and *kyrtos*, meaning 'humped.'"

In spring you'll find sassafras, *Sassafras albidum*, a deciduous tree whose roots are used to make

Toadlily, *Tricyrtis* 'Sinonome'

Bluestar, *Amsonia* 'Blue Ice'

Leadplant, *Amorpha canescens*

tea, root beer, and perfumes; Creole chefs grind its leaves to make filé powder for gumbo. First exported by Sir Walter Raleigh in 1602, it was extremely popular during the 17th century, when Europeans believed it could cure venereal diseases. There's also purple coneflower, *Echinacea purpurea*, and red switchgrass, *Panicum virgatum* 'Shenandoah,' a long prairie grass that comes up green with red tips in spring, adds pink flowers for summer, then finishes the year in a swoon of burgundy.

During spring and summer the bright purple meadow sage, *Salvia nemorosa*, and the low-growing bluestar, *Amsonia* 'Blue Ice,' dominate. Fall brings the incandescent gold of thread-leaf bluestar, *Amsonia hubrichtii*; the blue-purple flowers of the mounding aromatic aster, *Aster oblongifolius*, 'Raydon's Favorite' (*p.25*); purple bushclover, *Lespedeza thunbergii* 'Gibraltar'; the bright, neon pink spikes of *Persicaria amplexicaulis* 'Firetail'; black chokeberry, *Aronia melanocarpa* 'Viking'; and leadplant, *Amorpha canescens*. The plants vary in shape, height, color, texture, and scent, and there is much to delight the eye, even in the coldest winter months as they die in countless "interesting ways."

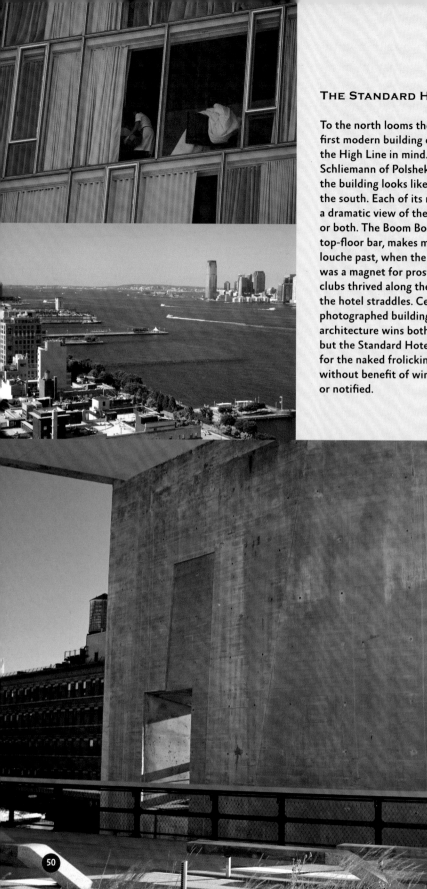

THE STANDARD HOTEL

To the north looms the Standard Hotel, the first modern building conceived specifically with the High Line in mind. Designed by Todd Schliemann of Polshek Partnership Architects, the building looks like a giant open book from the south. Each of its more than 300 rooms has a dramatic view of the city, the Hudson River, or both. The Boom Boom Room, the Standard's top-floor bar, makes much of the neighborhood's louche past, when the Meatpacking District was a magnet for prostitution and gay/BDSM sex clubs thrived along the streets and alleys that the hotel straddles. Certainly one of the most photographed buildings along the High Line, its architecture wins both accolades and disapproval; but the Standard Hotel is perhaps most notorious for the naked frolicking that some guests enjoy without benefit of window curtains. Be warned, or notified.

52 View of the High Line looking south from the Standard Hotel.

WHITNEY MUSEUM ON THE HIGH LINE

In 2015 the Whitney Museum of American Art will open the doors of its new building, designed by architect Renzo Piano, on Gansevoort between West Street and the High Line. The new structure will consist of more than 50,000 square feet of indoor galleries and 13,000 square feet of outdoor exhibition space. There will also be a theater, study center, research library, conservation lab, classrooms, and a multiuse black box theater for performance, film, video, and art installations. Adam D. Weinberg, the Whitney's director, has spoken of the museum as being "a bridge between the great open space of the Hudson River and the urban landscape of Manhattan, two of the great sources of inspiration for American artists."

Recognizing how difficult it was for American artists in the early 20th century to exhibit and sell their work, Gertrude Vanderbilt Whitney, a sculptor of international repute, opened the

Gertrude Vanderbilt Whitney with her assistant, Salvatore F. Bilotti, in her studio on MacDougal Alley, c.1939. At center is the maquette for her sculpture *Spirit of Flight*, which was exhibited at the 1939 World's Fair in New York.
Photo Walt Sanders, Black Star

Renderings of the Whitney Museum's new building designed by Renzo Piano, located in the Meatpacking District and scheduled to open in 2015. Courtesy Renzo Piano Building Workshop in collaboration with Cooper, Robertson & Partners.

Edward Hopper (1882–1967), *Early Sunday Morning*, 1930. Oil on canvas, 34¾ × 59⅝ in. (88.3 × 151.4 cm). Whitney Museum of American Art, New York; purchase with funds from Gertrude Vanderbilt Whitney 31.426

Whitney Studio in 1914 and dedicated herself to creating a space where living American artists could display pieces that had been disregarded by the established and more traditional academies and museums. After the Metropolitan Museum of Art turned down her increasingly large collection, in 1931 she established her own museum on 8th Street in Greenwich Village. It briefly moved to midtown in the 1950s but quickly outgrew that space. In 1966 the Whitney Museum of American Art opened its now-famous location on Madison Avenue and 75th Street, in a building designed by Marcel Breuer. Since then the collection has grown from some 2,000 pieces to more than 19,000. The new building returns the museum to its original downtown roots and creates a vast new exhibition space for old and new works.

The Whitney was a pioneer in bringing art to people who didn't go to museums. In the 1960s it was the first museum to venture outside its own walls to bring "the benefits of an awareness of art" into communities around the city.

Jasper Johns (b.1930), *Three Flags*, 1958. Encaustic on canvas, 30⅞ × 45½ × 5 in. (78.4 × 115.6 × 12.7 cm). Whitney Museum of American Art, New York; 50th Anniversary Gift of the Gilman Foundation, Inc., The Lauder Foundation, A. Alfred Taubman, Laura-Lee Whittier Woods, and purchase 80.32

The new building will engage with the High Line both architecturally and culturally, and will create an artistic anchor in a neighborhood already known for being one of the most vitally important arts centers in New York.

Metal Canopies and Belgian Block

The architecture of the Meatpacking District reflects the neighborhood's commercial history, and from the High Line it's easy to spot two of the area's distinctive features. Several of the buildings on 14th, Little West 12th, Washington, and Gansevoort Streets were owned by the Astor family in the 19th century and still retain the metal canopies that provided shelter from the weather to grocers and farmers who used these buildings and their street fronts as a giant outdoor market.

Belgian block paving — often mistaken for cobblestones — has been preserved on some of the streets, including Gansevoort and Little West 12th. Also called "setts," they are the same kind of stones found along the Champs-Élysées in Paris, more level than the rounder cobblestones but full of character.

Gansevoort–14th Streets

MANHATTAN REFRIGERATING COMPANY

From "West Side Improvement" brochure, New York Central Railroad, 1934.

In the late 1890s the Manhattan Refrigerating Company developed a complex system of underground pipes, 2,800 feet long, that brought refrigeration to cold-storage warehouses throughout the neighborhood. This pioneering technology had a major influence on the growth of both the food and shipping businesses in lower Manhattan, contributing to the area's prowess as both port and food distribution hub. Trains ran down the High Line and through the Manhattan Refrigerating Company warehouse on their way to or from the St. John's Terminal at Spring Street, the railroad's original terminus. At the turn of the century this huge warehouse was cooled with water from the Hudson River and had separate floors for fruit, vegetables, and meat. In those days the building had no windows, in order to keep the sun out and the interior cold. Today the former Manhattan Refrigerating warehouse is an apartment building called the West Coast.

P. F. Collier & Son Building

New York has long been the center of American
publishing, and the High Line runs through neighborhoods once filled with printing, binding, and
book publishing companies (*pp.154, 165*). Peter F.
Collier created the largest book-subscription house
in America, headquartered at 416–424 West 13th
Street. In 1888 he began publishing *Collier's Weekly,*
which became one of the best-selling magazines in
the country. Not only did it provide a forum for
turn-of-the-century muckraking journalists such as
Ida Tarbell, Ray Stannard Baker, and Upton Sinclair,
but it also gave the world the Gibson Girl and
Fu Manchu. The building was constructed in 1900
on Astor family land, and it came to be regarded as
one of the earliest examples of modern architecture
in New York City. In 1929, General Electric took
over the lease and until the 1970s used the former
Collier printing plant as a warehouse.

Pier 54

In a landscape so dominated by verticals and horizontals, the arched steel entryway to Pier 54 (at the foot of 13th Street) stands out along the Hudson River and makes a handsome contrast. Perhaps no other pier in America has so much history attached to it. Completed in 1910, it was designed by Warren & Wetmore, the architectural firm that co-designed Grand Central Terminal; two years later the *Carpathia* docked here to discharge survivors of the RMS *Titanic,* which had been heading for Pier 59. In May 1915 the *Lusitania* departed from Pier 54 and only days later was torpedoed by the Germans, an event that mobilized public opinion in support of the United States's entry into World War I. The pier was again pressed into service during World War II, when it was used for troopships. Today it's a venue for rock concerts and is a major party site during New York's annual Gay Pride celebration.

DVF Studio

The "diamond in the sky," as it has been called, is the private penthouse of fashion designer Diane von Furstenberg, famous for creating the iconic wrap dress. This distinctive geometric set of angled windows sits atop her company headquarters and store on Washington and 14th Streets. Computerized heliostat mirrors were installed in the dome to track the sun and reflect the maximum amount of natural light down the staircase at a constant angle. Along the staircase (which the architects, in their inimitable way, have branded a "stairdelier") are panels of glass made from more than 3,000 Swarovski crystal prisms that disperse the light. The penthouse was built in Spain and shipped in containers to lower Manhattan.

14TH STREET PASSAGE

The 14th Street Passage is a former warehouse and frozen-storage facility for the meatpacking industry. Today a new office tower at 450 West 14th Street rises above the old foundation. This is the only building along the High Line that shares the structure and support system of the original elevated railroad. Peer over the railing and you can see how the steel of the viaduct meets the brick and stone masonry of the building. A designer from the Morris Adjmi architectural firm stumbled upon a vivid reminder of the building's original use when he visited the basement before work commenced: around sixty enormous vats containing the remnants of animal carcasses.

A writer for the *Wall Street Journal* observed that "the north and south facades of the glass skyscraper bear four-story indentations, as though a giant pair of fingers had gently pressed in the glass."

2002 View of the wild High Line looking north from 26th Street.

THE WILD HIGH LINE

Two of the most commonly asked questions about the High Line are: *What was here when the place was wild?* and *What plants have been preserved in the modern gardens?* They are questions without perfect answers, but a bit of history helps us understand.

After the trains stopped running in 1980 a great variety of plants began to grow in the abandoned rail line, and it evolved into a wild garden. For some thirty years the old viaduct was in a constant state of change and evolution. Some plants that were observed ten or fifteen years ago are no longer growing, while new ones have sprung up to replace them. Almost half of the species on the wild High Line were native, meaning they naturally occur in New York, and the rest came from somewhere else. In 2004 the botanist Richard Stalter conducted a survey of flora on the High Line and encountered "a very high level of species richness." In scientific terms, what he found was 161 species of plants from 122 genera in 48 families.

According to Stalter, the plants got here in various ways. Some seeds, like little plant hoboes, were inadvertently transported to the High Line by trains that came from all over the country before the railroad was abandoned. Human trespassers introduced seeds of other plant species via the soles of their shoes, while birds carried them in on their feathers and left them in their droppings. Birds feed on the fruit of many plant species, and scientists now know that a bird's digestion process actually enhances seed germination. Stalter speculates that some species — including poison ivy, Virginia creeper, and black cherry — made their way to the High Line via bird droppings, while still other species, such as dandelion, milkweed, and goat's beard, *Tragopogon*, were carried here by the wind.

Wherever they came from — New York State, North America, Asia, Africa, or Europe — the plants along the old railroad arrived here in the way a great majority of Manhattanites did: as immigrants who managed to find a home among New York's canyons.

Today, in the still-wild portion near the old West Side Rail Yards, one can find dwarf bearded iris, garden chives, tree of heaven, sumac, and crabapple trees. Most distinctive of all, and marvelously visible from behind the temporary gate at 30th Street, are corridors of Queen Anne's lace, a plant of stunning delicacy and beauty that Joel Sternfeld captured in his early photos (*p.67*).

Joel Sternfeld, *A Railroad Artifact, 30th Street, May 2000*

Joel Sternfeld, *Looking West on 30th Street on a September Evening, 2000*

Joel Sternfeld, *A View Towards the Hudson, Late February 2001*

Joel Sternfeld, *Looking South on a May Evening
(the Starrett-Lehigh Building), May 2000*

JOEL STERNFELD

*Walking the rails is a rural experience, and here you
are in the middle of Manhattan. . . . Sometimes people
look at the pictures of the High Line and they think
that I've digitally altered [them] to put this beautiful
pathway through New York City. But there's nothing
digital about it. This is how it is up here, that's what
makes it so rare and so special. . . . This is just a magic
landscape that exists in space and time.*

— Joel Sternfeld

Perhaps the defining legacy of the High Line will
be the work of Joel Sternfeld, one of the country's
most respected landscape photographers. Sternfeld
was invited by Friends of the High Line to take
pictures of the abandoned railroad as part of its
effort to increase awareness and raise funds to save
the structure. As Elizabeth Barlow Rogers, founding president of the Central Park Conservancy,
recounts in an article for the journal *Sitelines*,
Robert Hammond took the photographer up to the
High Line one cold day in March 2000. Sternfeld
looked around, then turned back to Hammond.
"Please don't let anyone else come up here."

Joel Sternfeld, *Queen Anne's Lace, July 2001*

Joel Sternfeld, *A Peach Tree, October 2000*

Joel Sternfeld, *A View Towards the Empire State Building, November 2000*

Joel Sternfeld, *A Spring Evening, the Hudson, May 2001*

Sternfeld spent a year taking photographs that, as it turned out, would drive the vision of the entire project. He explained to Rogers that he only shot photos on days when the sky was a neutral gray. "I wanted it to be clear in the pictures that if there was glory in the High Line, it wasn't due to my skill as a photographer. By not borrowing beauty from the sky, the High Line itself is what is important in the picture." After Sternfeld's photographs were published they became a guiding force for the park's landscape architects and designers, who sought to preserve the spirit of wildness that his camera had captured.

So if the High Line has a muse it is Joel Sternfeld. Sternfeld himself was inspired by the 19th-century artist and photographer William Henry Jackson, who in 1870 was invited to join the U.S. government survey of the Yellowstone River and Rocky Mountains. As Sternfeld told a reporter, "For years there had been rumors of this fantastic region in the West with geysers and waterfalls, but nobody had seen Yellowstone until Jackson brought back the pictures. And as soon as he brought them back Congress made Yellowstone into a national park. In a way I feel like Jackson. . . . It's been the most extraordinary experience to be in the heart of New York City and see this secret landscape that only a few people have ever seen."

PIET OUDOLF
AND PLANTS OF THE HIGH LINE

Piet Oudolf, the Dutch landscape and planting designer who designed the High Line's gardens, wanted visitors to experience a journey as they walked through the park, so he created strikingly different environments constructed of plants that would be interesting in every season of the year. A grassland, a woodland thicket, a perennial meadow, a lawn, an open prairie, a bog: all "tell a story as you walk along." To Oudolf the whole

cycle of a plant's life should delight us, from the bright colors of the blooming season to the dry, spiky, seed-encrusted stalks of winter.

Oudolf selected some 250 species of perennials, grasses, shrubs, vines, and trees for the High Line. Many are native to North America, while others come from places as far away as Asia and Europe. His intention was to create a new landscape and at the same time preserve that spirit of wildness that had captivated so many early visitors to the abandoned High Line. As Oudolf once explained: "All of my work is

related to trying to recreate the spontaneous feeling of plants in nature. The idea is not to copy nature, but to give an emotion of nature."

Just as the garden of the abandoned railroad evolved and changed during the fifty years that it grew untended, so will the composition of plants in the cultivated gardens of the modern High Line. "A garden isn't a landscape painting that you look at but a dynamic process that's always changing," Oudolf told a reporter. "You must keep in touch with it all of the time."

Dying in an interesting way is just as important as living.
— Piet Oudolf

Yellow onion, *Allium obliquum*, and red clover, *Trifolium rubens,* are not commonly found in gardens in North America but are signature plants of Piet Oudolf's and are included in his list of "Dream plants for the natural garden." On the High Line they play a prominent role as Oudolf shows just how beautiful these plants can be.

HIGH LINE LIGHTS

As the sun sets, energy-efficient LED lights
designed by L'Observatoire International pop on;
all are below eye level, and they gently shine
on the plants and grasses, casting shadows through
the decorative rails and providing just enough
brightness to light the path.

ON THE HIGH LINE

14TH–16TH STREETS

Giant horsetail, *Equisetum hyemale*

Cattail, *Typha minima*

Smooth sumac, *Rhus glabra*

THE BOG

The island of Manhattan is at its widest point at 14th Street, which is also one of the widest parts of the High Line, an area where three trains could pass one another simultaneously. In the center, dividing the upper part of the park from the lower, is the High Line's bog, which contains plants that are all native to the United States and can be found in a wet area like a marsh, pond, or along a river's edge. In 2004, when a full ecological assessment was made of the old viaduct, the planners discovered a number of wet pockets in which water-loving plants like reeds and irises grow, including one just a few blocks north of the site of the current bog. While it's not the exact spot of the original bog, the High Line's designers placed it here "in homage to these areas that formed naturally years ago."

Because it is so wide and open this is also one of the windiest areas of the park, with gusts blowing across the plaza from both the east and the west. Only hardy plants — like the prairie grasses — can survive the wind shear that comes off the buildings. Sitting as it does thirty feet above sea level, the High Line consists of a series of microclimates. The horticultural staff deals with an odd and possibly unique situation: the park is one zone colder in winter and one zone warmer in summer.

In early spring the large five-petaled, bright pink flowers of Indian rhubarb bloom, and shortly thereafter the leaves open out and turn the plant into what looks like an inside-out umbrella (it's also known as umbrella plant).

Despite the fact that *Equisetum hyemale* is called giant horsetail, it is actually a modest-sized relative of a giant, ancient species of plants

that dominated forests during the Paleozoic era. It's a wonderfully expressive plant, a true living fossil, and it fulfills Piet Oudolf's vision that a plant should be interesting during all the cycles of its life. Its coarse bristles, once they have been boiled and dried, are used in Japan as a fine sandpaper and by musicians to finely shape and soften the reeds of a clarinet or saxophone.

The pickerelweed, *Pontederia cordata*, most likely got its name because it grows in the same habitat — shallow, vegetated waters of lakes, pools, and swamps — as the pickerel fish. And like the fish the whole plant is edible: the seeds can be eaten like nuts and the leaf stalks cooked as greens.

No bog would be complete without cattails, and there are two kinds here: the graceful *Typha laxmannii*, and a shorter, compact species,

There is also *Heuchera macrorhiza* 'Autumn Bride,' a low-growing plant with fuzzy, chartreuse leaves that is native to forest habitats in the Southeast. The willow-leaf spicebush, *Lindera glauca* var. *salicifolia*, is a shrub that turns vibrant apricot in autumn and then pales to a soft nutty brown, retaining its leaves throughout the winter. Mountain mint, *Pycnanthemum muticum*, thrives in the woods of the Northeast and has white flowers that attract butterflies and bees. Just the gentlest brush of its leaves releases a powerful, minty scent. Ohio goldenrod, *Solidago ohioensis,* grows in bogs and moist prairies and is among the showiest of the goldenrods; its wide-spreading yellow flowers brighten the fall landscape. Smooth sumac, *Rhus glabra*, is the only shrub or tree species that's native to all 48 contiguous states; it turns fiery red in the

THE PIER TRICK

The great travel writer Jan Morris, in her book *Manhattan '45,* shares the simple calculation that dockworkers used to locate a specific pier: subtract forty from the number of the pier and that's the nearest street where you'll find it. Hence the Circle Line, at Pier 83, can be found at the foot of 43rd Street.

PIERS AND PILE FIELDS

Up and down the Hudson River and visible from many places along the High Line are "pile fields," the remnants of piers that recall the early 19th century, when this was the busiest port in America. It supported a massive trading empire that stretched across the oceans to include South America, Spain, Portugal, England, and China. The piers may be long gone but the piles remain because they provide habitat for various fish species, including striped bass, flounder, Atlantic herring, American eel, white perch, and bay anchovy. They're also used by barnacles, clams, sea grapes, and shipworms, a form of mollusk that bores holes in the wood and eats the sawdust.

PIER 57

The Marine and Aviation Pier 57 is a structure in limbo. Built in 1952 to replace the French Line's wooden pier, which had been destroyed by a 1947 fire, the three-story behemoth is supported by floating concrete caissons. At the time it was built it was considered an engineering marvel; an executive of the Metropolitan Waterfront Alliance described it as "a lateral skyscraper laid down on its side." In 2004 it became known as "Guantanamo on the Hudson" after it was used as a holding center for people who were arrested — and held for as long as 24 hours — for protesting the Republican National Convention, which was being held in Madison Square Garden. It's currently used as a parking garage but is expected to be developed into a multimillion-dollar mixed-use park, public market, and entertainment facility.

14th–16th Streets

The Sun Deck

The sun deck, which extends between 14th and 15th Streets, is one of the most popular spots on the High Line. The lounge chairs are mounted on old rail ties, some with wheels so they can be moved together to accommodate large groups of friends or apart so lovers can separate themselves from the crowd. This is a great spot to experience the sunset and watch boat traffic along the Hudson River: tugs, freighters, cruise ships, police boats, yachts, kayaks, sailboats, ice breakers, the Circle Line, water taxis, Coast Guard skiffs, and even an occasional nautical celebrity like the environmental group Greenpeace's former sealing vessel, *Arctic Sunrise,* or the *Maltese Falcon,* one of the largest sailing yachts in the world. During warm weather a "water feature" blankets the pavers opposite the lounge chairs with a light scrim of water and creates a pleasant gurgling sound. Early in the morning, when the park first opens, sparrows claim this area as a giant birdbath. Later, packs of children arrive and transform it into a sidewalk pool.

Hoboken Terminal

The grand Hoboken Terminal was designed in the Beaux Arts style by Kenneth M. Murchison, with stained-glass windows by Louis Comfort Tiffany. It's considered one of the most beautiful and historically important transportation hubs in the country. Opened as a rail and ferry terminal in 1907 for the Delaware, Lackawanna and Western Railroad, the site has been in use since the colonial era, when it provided one of the main forms of access to Manhattan. Many movies have been filmed there, including *On the Waterfront*. At night the tower is lit and the words "ERIE LACKAWANNA" can be read from across the river.

The Liberty Inn

The triangular little building on 14th Street that is currently home to the Liberty Inn has a long, splendidly disreputable history. Opened in 1908 as the Strand Hotel, it was a boarding house for sailors and later, during Prohibition, became a speakeasy. Its most notorious period was as The Anvil, a gay club famous for its graphic go-go dancers. Felipe Rose, the "Indian" from the Village People, was discovered here. Beginning in 1970, a year after the Stonewall riots, a string of gay clubs and men's bathhouses opened along the West Side Highway, running down to Christopher Street in the Village and extending west to the deserted piers, long the heart of Manhattan's gay life and culture. The Anvil closed in 1985, a casualty of the AIDS crisis, but on its website the recently renovated Liberty Inn — the last remaining by-the-hour hotel in the neighborhood — still promises to welcome you at all hours with "Fast, discreet check-in service."

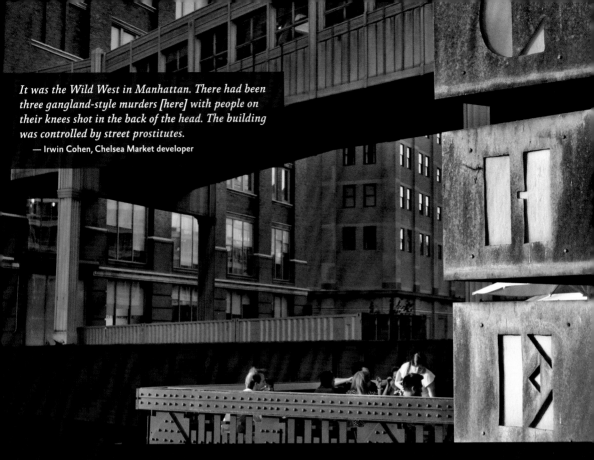

It was the Wild West in Manhattan. There had been three gangland-style murders [here] with people on their knees shot in the back of the head. The building was controlled by street prostitutes.
— Irwin Cohen, Chelsea Market developer

CHELSEA MARKET

The complex of twenty-two buildings that makes up the Chelsea Market was begun in the 1890s and completed in 1913 by the National Biscuit Company. Known today as Nabisco, this was the first of West Chelsea's start-up industries to become a major national corporation. The most prominent building — an eleven-story structure connected to the High Line by a train spur that sits below an enclosed pedestrian bridge — was erected on landfill that included the anchor, chain, and timbers of a two-masted schooner wreck found during excavation. An 1892 New York City guidebook notes there were forty ovens on site "of a capacity sufficient to convert 1,000 barrels of flour into biscuits of various sorts, every day." Until 1959, Nabisco created new systems here for packaging and advertising products that are as popular today as they were a hundred years ago: Premium Saltines, Fig Newtons, Barnum's Animal Crackers, Nilla Wafers, Oreo cookies, and the Mallomar.

The Chelsea Market opened for business in 1997 after years of being a derelict home to prostitutes and gangsters. And the ovens are still hot: a number of acclaimed bakeries are located here, but they're not the titans of yesteryear. Most of the merchants who have shops in today's Chelsea Market are small or medium-sized, local businesses that have some connection to food. A notable exception is Posman Books, one of the city's top independent bookstores. Companies with offices on the upper floors include corporate behemoths like Google, the Food Network, and EMI Music.

14th–16th Streets

WILDLIFE ON THE HIGH LINE

The Painted Lady is one of several types of butterfly that can be seen on the High Line. Many different birds have been spotted in the park, including woodpeckers, finches, mourning doves, house wrens, yellow warblers, song sparrows, and a peregrine falcon. More than 200 species of bees have been recorded in New York City, and many can be seen foraging along the High Line during the spring and summer months. Visitors have also reported hearing crickets, an odd sound in the midst of a bustling city. The Hudson River is a major migratory corridor for birds, and some 300 species — including songbirds, raptors, waterfowl, and shorebirds — pass through town each year on their northern migration.

The Porch

The Porch at 16th Street is a seasonal eatery that serves local food in the most sustainable way possible. In an effort to keep waste to a minimum the menu offerings are mostly hand-held and therefore don't require utensils. Herbal teas and local beer on tap are served in biodegradable paper cups, and food scraps are returned to the High Line's plants as compost. The establishment was designed to fulfill the Friends of the High Line mandate to educate visitors about green spaces and sustainability, ideas that inform virtually every aspect of the park from the choice of materials used in construction to plant selection and the design of the irrigation system.

View north from 14th Street toward the Southern Spur, which connects the High Line to the National Biscuit Company plant. From "West Side Improvement" brochure, New York Central Railroad, 1934.

THE SOUTHERN SPUR

The Southern Spur may seem a bit forlorn compared to its northern neighbor (*p.88*), which became an acclaimed horticultural preserve. But back in the day, both railway offshoots served the same essential purpose as all the other "spurs" along the elevated railroad: to enable manufacturers to receive and send goods quickly and inexpensively. Reducing the reliance on trucks, which slowed down the loading process only to become snarled in traffic later on, saved time and money and helped account for the railway's nickname: the "Life Line of New York." For decades trains carrying milk, eggs, and flour entered the National Biscuit Company via the Southern Spur, and out came cookies and crackers to feed a hungry nation.

Looking south across the Northern Spur to the Southern Spur, and beyond to the Hudson River and Statue of Liberty in the distance.

Astor Farmland

Much of the land in the Meatpacking District was originally owned by John Jacob Astor. In 1805 Astor paid George Clinton, governor of New York and later vice president of the United States, $75,000 for farmland called Greenwich Place. Properties in the neighborhood remained in the Astor family until the 1950s. Two surviving examples are the red brick buildings at 440 West 14th Street and 817–821 Washington Street (*p.57*). Both are "French Flats," apartments intended for middle-class tenants that were considered superior to the tenements where the working class lived. These buildings have distinctive metal canopies that protected the merchants who worked in street-level shops from the elements. Along 14th Street, between the High Line and Ninth Avenue, several original factory buildings still stand,

including a former brewery, a print works, and a carpenter's shop. Over the centuries the neighborhood has been home to a wide diversity of businesses including fancy fruit importers, fine arts and photography studios, telegraph firms, and makers of cosmetics, furniture, cigars, upholstery, carpets, marine supplies, sporting goods, butchers' tools, electronics, and more.

Merchants Refrigerating Building

The Northern Spur provided access to the Merchants Refrigerating Company Warehouse, a giant cold-storage facility. It was built in 1917 and only later, in the 1930s, was retrofitted to accommodate the rail tracks. Cold storage was an important innovation of the early 20th century, and warehouses like this one allowed vast quantities of meat, seafood, fish, poultry, and vegetables to be delivered to lower Manhattan, stored for a time, and then reshipped around the country later on. When the warehouse was closed in 1983 the developer who purchased it told a reporter that it took seven months for the entire building to thaw. All the windows that are visible from the High Line were installed after the structure reopened as an office building. Today it houses numerous governmental agencies including the Drug Enforcement Agency.

THE NORTHERN SPUR

This is Oudolf's signature, a meticulous but layered as-God-would-strew-it planting algorithm.
— Guy Martin, *The Observer*

The viewing stand overlooking the Northern Spur Horticultural Preserve, between 16th and 17th Streets, is a fine spot from which to observe the wide range of wild vegetation that sprang up here after the railroad was closed in 1980. Here the High Line's gardeners planted a variety of native grasses and perennials to recall the "self-sown" landscape that emerged after the trains stopped running.

THE RIVER THAT FLOWS BOTH WAYS

The inaugural exhibit in the Chelsea Passage is one artist's attempt to quite literally capture the color of water. Spencer Finch spent nearly twelve full hours during the course of a single day photographing the Hudson River, minute by minute, from a tugboat. His installation of 700 images, each of which contains a single pixel of color captured from the water's surface, pays tribute to the tidal power of the river, which was first named by the Mahican Indians *Muh-he-kun-ne-tuk,* variously translated as "where waters were never still" or "the river that flows both ways." During a very cold winter it's easy to see how the river — which is actually a tidal estuary — got its name, as huge chunks of ice appear to drift simultaneously "both ways," up the river and down.

Spencer Finch, *The River That Flows Both Ways*, 2009. Installation of 700 panes of colored glass. Presented by Creative Time, Friends of the High Line, and the New York City Department of Parks & Recreation.

THE LOW ROAD

The path of the tracks bifurcates at 16th Street, offering pedestrians an opportunity to follow the route the dairy trains once took as they veered onto the Southern Spur to make deliveries to the Nabisco building. On the lower level there's a lovely spot with bistro chairs and tables — a park within a park — where visitors can sit and watch the world go by. At night the entire passage is cast in blue light (*p.92*), making it a quiet, romantic oasis. Before the High Line opened this passage was a "guerrilla art gallery" (*pp.138, 192*) as one reporter described it, "crammed with graffiti murals by some of New York's legends . . . [and] an illegal iron installation welded to a steel beam."

View down Tenth Avenue from 17th Street of the
Chelsea Passageway and Northern and Southern Spurs.

Courtesy Kalmbach Publishing Co.

THE LAST TENTH AVENUE COWBOY

Since the 1999 establishment of Friends of the High Line — the "rusty trestle's very own fashionable 501 (c)(3)"— made the park an international *cause célèbre,* the story of the West Side Cowboy has become embedded in the High Line's narrative.

The job of urban cowboy was created by an 1850s city ordinance that permitted freight cars to run along the streets so long as they didn't exceed six miles per hour and dictated that the railroad — first the Hudson River, later the New York Central — "shall employ a proper person to precede the trains on horseback, to give the necessary warning in a suitable manner on their approach." Still, so many accidents and deaths occurred on the at-grade tracks along Tenth Avenue between 17th and 30th Streets that it came to be known as "Death Avenue." The "proper persons" were the West Side Cowboys; they waved a red flag by day and a red

lantern by night to give their necessary warning.

New York's urban cowboys figured in Mario Puzo's 1965 novel, *The Fortunate Pilgrim,* in which they were known as "dummy boys." A scene in the novel, which is set in the Hell's Kitchen neighborhood where Puzo grew up, describes two boys gazing out their childhood window: "Far down Tenth Avenue they could see the red lantern of a dummy boy and behind it, like a small round ghost, the white dot of the trailing engine searchlight."

It was at 10:50 a.m., not high noon, that the last cowboy rode down Tenth Avenue. It was March 29, 1941. He was George Hayde, age twenty-one, mounted on what one reporter dubbed "his faithful bay, Cyclone." The two led a string of fourteen freight cars loaded with oranges.

The team of reporters that covered the event agreed afterward that George and Cyclone had completed the trip without exceeding the speed limit.

The horses used in this unusual service are tried and true, and are perfectly aware of their important mission in life. They know traffic and excitement, thick fogs and blinding storms, the deep-throated adieus of departing liners and the tremendous thrill of screaming fire engines, but through it all they move surely and serenely, carrying out the Law of the City Council and giving opportunity for their gallant riders to amuse the passerby with amazing variation of the routine waving of the red lanterns. The effective term of duty of these mounts for this service is over eight years . . . and when their usefulness on the city pavements is over they are auctioned off at the Bulls Head Horse Market to continue their lives on softer turf in greener pastures.

— from "Cowboys of the Cobblestones"
London Terrace *Tatler*, January 1934

Larry Angeluzzi spurred his jet-black horse proudly through a canyon formed by two great walls of tenements, and at the foot of each wall, marooned on their separate blue-slate sidewalks, little children stopped their games to watch him with silent admiration. He swung his red lantern in a great arc; sparks flew from the iron hoofs of his horse as they rang on railroad tracks, set flush in the stones of Tenth Avenue, and slowly following horse, rider, and lantern, came the long freight train, inching its way north from St. John's Park terminal on Hudson Street.

— Mario Puzo
The Fortunate Pilgrim, 1965

"DEATH AVENUE" AMPHITHEATER

The bleachers of the High Line's amphitheater provide a priceless "only in New York" moment, for where else would a theater be constructed with a grand view of traffic in motion? Tourists and natives alike perch here day and night with their cups of coffee to enjoy the endless rumble of trucks, taxis, cars, limos, bicycles, and motorized scooters as they make their way down the road formerly known as "Death Avenue" (*p.94*). Traffic has always been an event in New York, and this stadium offers a fine — and uniquely stress-free — way to experience and indeed appreciate the unending vehicular flow as an art form unto itself.

16th–20th Streets

the sooner you park your car,
the sooner you can stop thinking
about parking your car.

View from the Tenth Avenue Square, looking north up Tenth Avenue.

TENTH AVENUE SQUARE

A signature quality of the High Line is the diversity of building materials that were used to transform the old railroad into a 21st-century park. One section, known as the Tenth Avenue Square, breaks from the concrete planking system and employs instead a Brazilian hardwood, ipê, to create a seating area amid a lovely grove of maple trees, *Acer triflorum*. There are stunning views here to the south — particularly at sunset — of the Statue of Liberty and New York Harbor. The change in materials also signals a transition from the strictly linear, enclosed tunnel of the Chelsea Passage to a curving, wide-open plaza with vast, sun-filled spaces just north of 17th Street. This is also, if you are in need, the location of the High Line's restroom.

ACER TRIFLORUM – MAPLE TREES

The trees in the Tenth Avenue Square are trifoliate maple, *Acer triflorum,* a native of northern China and Korea, which in North America is rarely found outside botanical gardens. Its papery, exfoliating bark is the color of tarnished brass. Most of the plants and trees along the High Line are planted in beds that are just 18 inches deep, with the exception of 36-inch beds for the birch trees in the Gansevoort Woodland area. If the High Line's gardeners need to gain access to the roots of these maples they can simply lift up the decking, which forms an almost invisible, removable box around each tree.

16th–20th Streets

ARCHITECTURE ON THE HIGH LINE

One of the great delights of the High Line is the mix of architectural styles that represent virtually every period of the city's history. New York, as the authors of *Gotham: A History of New York City to 1898* put it, is "a perpetual work-in-progress," and the High Line is a great, unfolding gallery where this urban work of art can be viewed in real time. The Tenth Avenue Square and Chelsea Grasslands offer some of the best and most dramatic views, including those of Frank Gehry's undulating IAC building —

often referred to as "the sail building" — and its starkly contrasting neighbor, the Chelsea Nouvel, with its multicolored windows, inset at varying angles and framed in steel, designed by architect Jean Nouvel.

So many new buildings by famous architects started popping up around the middle section of the High Line that the area became known as "architects row." As they drew up their plans, the designers of 459 West 18th Street, an angular white and black building, considered the design of the condominium next door, farther from the park,

with its undulating blue and white windows. They wanted the geometry, colors, and surface textures of both structures to complement each other. The result is a pair of frequently photographed buildings that's fascinating to look at in every type of light.

The Metal Shutter Houses on 19th Street, just to the east of the IAC headquarters, has a constantly changing façade, depending on decisions made by the people who live there. Designed by Shigeru Ban, a Japanese architect best known for his work creating temporary shelters for people who have lost their homes during natural disasters and wars, the building consists of nine duplex apartments that feature motorized metal shutters, that can be raised or lowered by residents to regulate sunlight and to ensure — or abandon — privacy. The exterior roll-up blinds were conceived to echo the ubiquitous after-hours shutters on galleries and bodegas around the neighborhood.

A bit to the east is the Maritime Hotel, which was designed in the 1960s around a nautical theme — porthole windows included — for the National Maritime Union of America.

New York is notoriously the largest and least loved of any of our great cities.
Why should it be loved as a city? It is never the same city for a dozen years together.
A man born in New York forty years ago finds nothing, absolutely nothing,
of the New York he knew.

— *Harper's Monthly*, 1856

View of of the High Line from Tenth Avenue at 18th Street, with (*from left*) Frank Gehry's IAC headquarters, Annabelle Selldorf's 520 West Chelsea, and Jean Nouvel's Chelsea Nouvel rising behind.

16th–20th Streets

TENEMENT HOUSES

Amid so much new construction by the so-called "starchitects," two small buildings on opposite sides of 17th Street stand as fine examples of the tenements that were abundant in this neighborhood during the 19th century; they provided housing for the mostly immigrant laborers and dockworkers who began coming to New York in waves beginning in the 1840s and worked in the many factories and warehouses in Chelsea and the Meatpacking District. These two buildings were erected in the 1880s after the passage of New York's first housing reform laws, which required, among other things, that buildings have fire escapes and that every room have a window that faces a source of fresh air and light. Unlike contemporary lower- and middle-class housing, these buildings each have handsome architectural details on their façades.

A TRAIN'S-EYE VIEW

Even lifelong New Yorkers marvel at the unusual point of view — about three stories above street level — that the High Line provides. It's not the soaring view of Manhattan that you get from a skyscraper, and yet it offers a 360-degree embrace of everything in sight: much more than you could ever see from even the grandest of picture windows. Thus, small architectural details can now be admired from a matter of mere yards, so much closer than the architect originally conceived. Call it a train's-eye view.

16th–20th Streets

Robert Adams, *Nebraska State Highway 2, Box Butte County, Nebraska,* 1978. Image installed in 2011 as a billboard (25 x 75 ft) near the High Line on West 18th Street. Presented by Friends of the High Line and the New York City Department of Parks & Recreation, courtesy Matthew Marks Gallery, New York, and Fraenkel Gallery, San Francisco. Photo Scott Mlyn.

Kim Beck, *Space Available,* 2011. Three sculptures installed on rooftops along Washington Street, presented by Friends of the High Line and the New York City Department of Parks & Recreation, courtesy of Mixed Greens NYC. Photo Bill Orcutt.

HIGH LINE ART

When the High Line opened in 2009 it did so with an uncommon dedication to public art. Friends of the High Line, the group that saved and oversaw the design of the elevated park, employs a full-time curator, and over the years commissions have included works in a wide variety of mediums, including music, photography, dance, landscape painting, sculpture, sound performance, and even roving food carts. All the exhibits are temporary with the exception of Spencer Finch's enduring Hudson River tribute, *The River That Flows Both Ways,* a piece in the Chelsea Passage *(p.90).*

The High Line extends through a neighborhood that has long been an important creative center for the visual arts, design, dance, theater, and performance. From the beginning, Friends of the High Line believed it was important that the park also become a cultural center, and that educational and entertainment programs for both children and adults take place throughout the year.

Opposite: **Sarah Sze,** *Still Life with Landscape (Model for a Habitat),* 2011, stainless steel, wood, 9 x 22 x 21 ft. Presented by Friends of the High Line and the New York City Department of Parks & Recreation. Photo Sarah Sze.

VESTIGES OF THE OLD RAILROAD

Meat Hooks
One can still see a handful of meatpacking trucks and men in blood-covered aprons in the streets below the High Line. Near the Standard Hotel, on the west side of the park, a series of old, rusting meat hooks hangs outside a former warehouse loading dock. The large hooks were attached to a pulley system that ran up and down a steel rod between the tracks and the warehouse. The trains of the High Line would pull up to this spot to deliver or receive their cargo.

Signal Lights
Multicolored signal lights guided trains along the High Line and regulated the flow of traffic. One set can still be found at the northern entrance to the Chelsea Passage at 17th Street.

Rail Ties
During the remediation of the old railbed and construction of the park, all the original rail ties placed here by the New York Central Railroad in the early 1930s were removed and tagged, and many were replaced in their original locations.

THE CHELSEA PIERS

The Chelsea Piers, which formally opened in 1910, was heralded by the *New York Times* as "one of the most remarkable waterfronts in the history of municipal improvements." The piers were first used as a passenger ship terminal for luxury ocean liners like the *Mauretania,* the *Lusitania,* the *Queen Elizabeth,* and the *Ile de France,* famous for being the most beautifully decorated ship in the world. Designed by Warren & Wetmore, the co-architects of Grand Central Terminal, the

The RMS Lusitania at Chelsea Piers depicted in a 1910 postcard.

monolithic complex consisted of a series of buildings that were connected by a massive pink-granite façade. To board, travelers passed through a huge arched entryway to reach the 800-foot-long piers that had been designed expressly for the modern age of luxury transatlantic travel. The piers were used during both World Wars to greet troopships, and in July 1936 exuberant crowds of well-wishers gathered to celebrate the departure of Jesse Owens and the United States Olympic team aboard the ocean liner *Manhattan,* which carried them to Berlin for the Summer Games. The Chelsea Piers were modernized for cargo ships in the 1960s and, to the dismay of many, the beautiful Beaux Arts façade, long considered an architectural masterpiece, was destroyed. Some thirty years later the site reopened as the Chelsea Piers sports and entertainment complex.

ARCHITECTURAL AND DESIGN ELEMENTS

Benches
The "peel-up" benches along the High Line are made from sustainably forested ipê, a South American tropical hardwood, and precast concrete.

Decorative Railings
Among the finest elements of the High Line's original design are the geometric shapes of the guardrails. The railroad's architects placed the elegant diamond- and square-patterned railings at street crossings only, where they could be appreciated by pedestrians . Where they were hidden by buildings, more prosaic steel pipes and concrete were used instead. During restoration, the railings were painted "Greenblack," a Sherwin-Williams color that combines black with a touch of green.

Expansion Joints
The High Line is, in essence, one long, giant bridge. To coordinate the movement of the old and new structures and allow them to absorb the seasonal shifts caused by thermal expansion, the engineers incorporated expansion joints into the concrete paving system that runs the length of the park.

Stone Mulch
The stone mulch on the High Line was selected because it resembles railroad ballast, the crushed rocks that are packed around rail ties to help distribute the load and facilitate drainage. It may have aesthetic integrity but it's not ideal for a garden: the stones get very hot in summer and the sharp, angular edges — ideal in the railbed because they interlock and therefore inhibit track

movement — can pierce the stems of plants. The stones have to be moved in order for the gardeners to dig, and this is partly why the High Line garden staff developed a "compost tea," which can be poured through the stones.

Pavers

A specially designed modular planking system constructed from precast concrete is used throughout the High Line. Some of the pavers are straight and some are tapered at the ends so that the plantings can push up around them, recreating the wild, "self-sown" feel of the park. The paving system was designed to expand and contract in concert with the structural bones of the former railway and to create what the High Line's architect describes as a "meandering, unscripted movement."

Drainage and Irrigation

An invisible but impressive drainage system was devised for the unique requirements of the High Line gardens, which for the most part consist of extremely shallow planting beds. Sometimes described as "the world's longest green roof," the park employs a complex mix of plastic "egg-crate" drainage panels and layers of crushed pea-gravel, woven filter fabric, clay subsoil, nutrient-rich topsoil, and gravel mulch. The pathways were designed to reduce the runoff of rainwater and strategically funnel it to the beds. And this being New York, the plants are well fed: they're fertilized with a special compost tea, a mix of decayed vegetation, natural fish fertilizer, and molasses or flour, which provides food for bacteria. The special concoction is stewed overnight in an aerated brewer before being spread around the plants.

GRASSES *by Rick Darke*

The High Line would be unrecognizable without its grasses. They contribute more to the essential character and dynamic qualities of its landscape than any other group of plants. Instead of brightly colored, broad-petaled flowers, the unique appeal of grasses is derived from texture, line, and form; sound, scent, and movement; and perhaps most of all, translucency. On the High Line, grasses are the matrix into which almost all else is set. Their soft texture and fine lines are perfect foils for architecture, furniture, and the comparatively coarse flowers, foliage, and seed heads of other plants. Grasses are the first to tell of every summer breeze. Their supple stalks flutter, bend, and bow, dancing to every storm, painting portraits of the wind. As they move they sing in tones ranging from a rustle to a low rattle. Their highly translucent flowers and foliage are readily set aglow by sunlight or moonlight, creating luminous displays that are especially dramatic when grasses are side lit or backlit. Scent isn't common among grasses, but when present it can be a delightful surprise. Few visitors fail to notice the unusual scent of prairie dropseed, *Sporobolus heterolepis*, which fills the late summer air on the High Line with a fragrance often likened to burnt buttered popcorn or crushed fresh cilantro.

In the ecological scheme of things, grasses are pioneers. They're always among the first species to colonize exposed sites, and due to their prolific capacity for self-seeding and their long-lived nature, they typically occur in masses. The iconic North American prairies are classic examples of landscapes dominated by grasses with a minor complement of intermingled broad-leaved plants. Piet Oudolf employed grasses extensively on the High Line in deliberate reference to these patterns.

The majority of the High Line's grasses are perennial, warm-season types, and warm-season

grasses like it hot. Their physiology is such that they grow best and fastest when soil temperatures rise above 70°F and air temperatures exceed 80°F. The result is that the High Line's grasses are slow to start in spring and have little height or presence until late May or June. Until then the vegetation along the Line is generally low, the tracks are still visible, and spring-flowering broad-leaved plants carry the day. Grasses achieve their full height and mass by August, and by this time their growth has literally transformed the scale of the landscape. Grasses are also directly responsible for the most dramatic changes in the High Line's seasonal color. The pervasive greens and blue-greens of summer are replaced in autumn by an array of golds, oranges, blue-purples, and burgundies, followed by a subtler but still colorful winter palette of fawn, chestnut, and russet. The sun's low angle in late autumn and winter further accentuates the radiant qualities of the grasses, contributing a welcome vibrancy to the landscape when typical flowering plants are at their lowest ebb.

Breaking the Grid

In 1811 the New York State Legislature adopted a plan to impose a grid on New York City, putting an end to the historically inchoate, willy-nilly character of the street design that had defined the city since its beginnings. The reasons were varied. At a time when yellow fever ran rampant through the city, the authorities believed that parallel, open streets and avenues would permit air circulation and therefore promote good health. But, showing an early passion for the business of real estate, the commissioners also noted that "strait-sided and right-angled houses are the most cheap to build," and the numbered streets would make properties easier to market for both buyers

Automobile Row

West Chelsea has a seemingly high ratio of automobiles to humans, and besides being famous for its architecture, art galleries, nightclubs, restaurants, and the High Line, the neighborhood is also notable for being a relatively easy place to park, repair, gas up, wash, or purchase a luxury car. Even the sun deck, one of the park's most dreamy spots, sits atop the mammoth Oil Change Center. Ten or so blocks north and in sight of the High Line on 25th Street is Tesla Motors, founded by a group of Silicon Valley engineers who, according to the company website, "set out to prove that electric vehicles could be awesome." Eleventh Avenue in West Chelsea is known as "Automobile Row" and is home to many luxury dealerships, some of which display orchids in the lobby, serve free cappuccino, and include an off-road track on the roof, complete with obstacle course.

and sellers. The most powerful — and colorful — objections came from Clement Clarke Moore, the wealthy proprietor of Chelsea, a huge estate of open fields and orchards that extended north from 20th to 28th Streets. Moore didn't exactly invent the modern celebration of Christmas, but he wrote its defining playbook, "A Visit From St. Nicholas" ("'Twas the night before Christmas when all through the house . . . "). He was enraged when Ninth Avenue, part of the new grid, cut through his property, and he accused the commissioners of catering to the influential lobbyists of the time: "cartmen, carpenters, masons, pavers, and all their host of attendant laborers." In response, the commissioners agreed to implement the grid only above 14th Street and east of Sixth Avenue.

Having also railed against the city for being forced to pay taxes to fund construction of the grid — "a tyranny no monarch in Europe would dare to exercise" — Moore nevertheless jumped on the real estate bandwagon himself and within a few years began developing his newly gridded-out property. It's perhaps symbolic, then, that just as the High Line begins its run through Moore's former estate in Chelsea it breaks from its strict linearity to jog a bit west at 17th Street, cutting a diagonal across the grid before continuing north in a straight path once again. This is also the southern end of the Special West Chelsea District that was created in 2007 as a means of preserving and protecting the High Line.

16th–20th Streets

VEGETAL WALL

Clematis and honeysuckle grow along the vegetal wall near 17th Street. These flowering vines add a lovely, sinuous, and strictly vertical horticultural element to the park, but they also have a practical purpose: they help screen the inevitable construction project that will go up in what's currently a large parking lot below.

CHELSEA GRASSLANDS

Chelsea Grasslands features a variety of interwoven grasses, including the complete cast of what the Lady Bird Johnson Wildflower Center calls "The Big Four." These are the native warm-season grass species that characterized the great North American prairies, which once covered the vast interior of the United States. They are familiar to anyone who loves Westerns or grew up reading *Little House on the Prairie*: big bluestem, *Andropogon gerardii,* also known as turkeyfoot, high in protein and much loved by horses and cattle; Indiangrass, *Sorghastrum nutans,* which has broad, blue-green blades and is resilient against flooding and frequent wildfires; switchgrass, *Panicum virgatum,* which is covered with lacy sprays of purple flowers in autumn; and little bluestem, *Schizachyrium scoparium,* which is a slate gray-blue in the growing season and then turns orange-red in fall. Another favorite, prairie dropseed, *Sporobolus heterolepis*, is a low-growing, very fine-textured grass that's responsible for the strong scent of cilantro that wafts throughout the High Line's grasslands in late summer. After the flowers have gone the seeds mature and provide a favorite feast for birds.

16th–20th Streets

Manhattan's Prison

On Eleventh Avenue at 20th Street is the Bayview Correctional Facility, a medium-security women's prison. In the 1930s the facility was part of the YMCA and was known as the Seaman's House; it offered beds to merchant sailors whose ships were docked at the piers. It's a fine building with decorative Art Deco engravings on the outside and stained-glass windows depicting seafaring motifs on the inside. Before the Jean Nouvel condominium went up next door there was a popular mural on the south side of the building called *Venus,* painted by artist Knox Martin. When news came that the condo would cover up the much-loved work, the artist, then eighty-three, told the *New York Times*: "I've seen it from a jet. It was like a song." The chain-link fence that's visible on the roof of Bayview cordons off the area where inmates go to smoke, play volleyball, or enjoy the flower garden.

The Life Savers Building

Across the street from the Bayview Correctional Facility is the former headquarters of the Mint Products Company, manufacturer of Life Savers mints, which were invented in 1912 by the father of poet Hart Crane. In the 1980s the building was home to The Spike, an infamous gay club; today it's a small, expensive condominium that houses, on the ground floor, a museum-gallery devoted to the work of author, sculptor, and pioneer of information design Edward Tufte.

GENERAL THEOLOGICAL SEMINARY

The land for General Theological Seminary — originally an apple orchard — was a gift from Chelsea landowner Clement Clarke Moore, who was the son of the Episcopal bishop of the Diocese of New York. Moore himself taught at General and also compiled the first Hebrew lexicon in America. It's the oldest Episcopal seminary in the country and was designed to resemble a traditional English university with a campus of neo-Gothic buildings embracing a large quadrangle, still referred to as the Close. When it was built in the 1820s the Hudson River flowed by the western edge of the building (and underneath the modern High Line), where a conference center honoring Desmond Tutu now stands. Three times a day the seminary's Guild of Chimers rings fifteen tubular bells — the oldest of their kind in the United States — to call the community to worship. The library at General houses the greatest collection of Latin Bibles in the world and includes a prized Gutenberg Bible. In 2008 the seminary installed a state-of-the-art geo-thermal heating and cooling system through which water is pumped from a depth of 1,500 feet — almost the height of the Empire State Building.

Compass plant, *Silphium laciniatum*

Prairie dock, *Silphium terebinthinaceum*

MORE OF PIET OUDOLF'S FAVORITES

The compass plant, *Silphium laciniatum*, is a prairie
flower that's commonly found along railroad
beds. This tall, yellow member of the aster family
resembles a wild sunflower and got its name from
the pioneers who originally settled the American
Heartland. They believed that its flowers — which
typically point in a north-south direction to enable
the plant to get as much sun as possible during the
course of the day — could be used as a compass.
Reaching for the sun, the compass plant often
grows as high as ten feet. On the High Line it frequently leans over the railings and makes a show of
its bright yellow flowers to pedestrians below.
Often, when it gets too tall, the flowering stems
topple and become nearly prostrate, but the individual flowers inevitably turn again, upward toward
the sun. Don't depend on it to replace your GPS,
but it's a beautiful plant to behold when it blooms
in midsummer.

A close relative of the compass plant is prairie
dock, *Silphium terebinthinaceum*, which also has
yellow flowers but is striking for its elephantine
green leaves. Both of these plants are popular with
birds; as with large sunflowers, the spent stalks

of *Silphium* stand tall and provide a great foraging
opportunity for many kinds of birds throughout
the winter months.

Other notable plants in and around the
Chelsea Grasslands include *Iris fulva*, a plant with
copper, red, or orange petals that's normally found
in moist areas like swampy woodlands, ditches,
or ponds in the Deep South. The long-blooming
pincushion plant, *Knautia macedonica* 'Mars
Midget,' can be found around the sun deck as well
as in the Chelsea Grasslands from July through
December.

Like so many plants on the High Line the
prairie blazing star, *Liatris pycnostachya*, is often
found growing along railroads. It's named after the
Greek word for "crowded" — *pycnostachya* —
because the flowers are arranged in dense clusters
along the long stalks.

The rattlesnake master, *Eryngium yuccifolium*,
is a prairie species that got its name from Native
Americans and pioneers who believed its roots were
an antidote to rattlesnake venom. Amerindians
used the dried seeds in rattles. In summer you will
find *Lythrum alatum*, the winged loosestrife that
Piet Oudolf has praised for its "jolly" spikes of
bright red and purple flowers.

Winter aconite, *Eranthis hyemalis,* is one of the very first plants to brighten the landscape, blooming in late winter before spring has arrived. It's a simple buttercup, but beware: lovely as it is, every part of this plant is poisonous.

Baffling as it may be to nonprofessionals, sometimes there's good reasoning behind the botanical nomenclature of plants. A case in point: *Hakonechloa macra* 'Aureola.' The genus name *Hakonechloa* is derived from Mt. Hakone, the Japanese mountain region where this grass grows, and *chloa,* the Greek word for grass. Its leaves are golden with green stripes, and in the fall they are strongly suffused with reddish pink. Unlike the taller, spikier prairie grasses from the American Midwest, the leaves of this Asian plant cascade to the ground. Along with grasses and plants native to many other foreign lands, including the British Isles, Europe, South America, and North Africa, this grass helps make the High Line a truly global park.

Two of Piet Oudolf's favorite plants that are truly unique elements in the High Line's plantings are the Siberian catmint, *Nepeta sibirica,* 'Souvenir d'André Chaudron,' and the bright yellow yarrow. The catmint adds its remarkable rich purple-blue to the High Line in May and June and is a feature of the Northern Spur. The yellow platters of the yarrow stand tall above masses of grasses in July and August. After flowering is finished, the sturdy seed heads remain standing and turn tawny, a feature of the High Line well into winter.

In abundance around the High Line is the bright yellow daffodil *Narcissus* 'Intrigue.' But look very hard in the northern end of the Chelsea Grasslands, on the west side of the park, and you might get lucky and catch sight of the *Narcissus* 'Rip Van Winkle,' a volunteer that snuck its way into a flat of other plants to the surprise of the gardening staff. One of the first blooms of spring, this flower takes its name from the sleepy character created by Washington Irving, who, among his other literary flights cofounded the satirical journal *Salmagundi,* which coined the nickname "Gotham" for New York City. (It also poked fun at then-President Thomas Jefferson, calling him "a huge bladder of wind.") In his famous satire of New York City, *Knickerbocker's History,* Washington wrote about "Sancte Clause," whose chimney antics were later appropriated by Chelsea author Clement Clarke Moore in "A Visit From St. Nicholas."

Hakone grass, *Hakonechloa macra*

Siberian catmint, *Nepeta sibirica,* 'Souvenir d'André Chaudron'

Yellow yarrow, *Achillea. Below:* Daffodil, *Narcissus* 'Rip Van Winkle'

ASTILBE, ALLIUM MT. EVEREST, STAGHORN SUMAC

Chinese astilbe, *Astilbe chinensis*, is a gorgeous plant that's unusually tolerant of sun and prospers even in the wide-open plaza of the Tenth Avenue Square. The robust sweet black-eyed Susan, *Rudbeckia subtomentosa*, also thrives in the hot New York City sun while so many other flowers fade away. There are two members of the allium — or garlic — family on the High Line: the drumstick *Allium sphaerocephalon*, which has an egg-shaped flower that stands tall and blooms bright pink, and the marvelous ornamental onion, *Allium* 'Mt. Everest.' It has a large, round white globe, and thanks to its height — from which it doubtless gets its name — is impossible to miss, even from street level.

Sumacs, hardy shrubs that will grow just about anywhere, were for generations not deemed garden-worthy. Many gardeners consider it a weed or confuse it with poison sumac. But staghorn sumac, *Rhus typhina*, with its great leaves and fuzzy stems that resemble the new antlers of a stag, has earned its place on the High Line alongside many more refined plants that get all the publicity and dominate the photo blogs. Some Native American tribes mix the leaves and berries of the staghorn sumac with herbs and smoke it during tribal council ceremonies, and it can also be used to make tea.

UGLY AND BEAUTIFUL

*The ugliness of New York is instantly amenable
to a mental flip-flop that converts it into beauty.*
— Phillip Lopate, *Waterfront*

Unique among New York City parks, the High Line
offers views that are almost pastoral in their natural
beauty alongside rusting industrial relics and
the ratty detritus of commercial activity. Art sits
next to commerce, industry aside entertainment.
And into the mix are thrown an Episcopal Seminary,
a women's prison, a trapeze school, and a seemingly
infinite number of parking garages.

ON THE HIGH LINE

20TH–23RD STREETS

THE HIGH LINE, PART TWO

On June 7, 2011, without fanfare and almost two years to the day of the anniversary of the original opening, the metal gate that had divided the park in half at 20th Street was removed and visitors entered part two of the High Line, where they encountered a new and quite different experience.

The northern half of the park feels less expansive than the southern; it's more hemmed in by buildings and runs through a markedly domestic environment — right by, and often under, the windows of lofts, condominiums, and apartments. The neighborhood is grittier and less gentrified than the Meatpacking District or lower Chelsea, though change is coming fast. Still, despite the fact that many of the converted factories are packed to the rafters with art galleries — some of which have tacked on fancy modifiers to their addresses like "+ Art," or "Creative" — in the northern section the typical sound track is men at work: a crane operator banging around in a scrap-metal yard or an auto-repair mechanic removing lug nuts with an air gun. At 24th Street a shiny new condo looks down on a gas station. A few blocks north a Mercedes Benz is visible through the top floor of an auto body shop that now occupies a former tenement building.

CONTAGION

Residences
available now

Chelsea Thicket

There are several pronounced areas of transition
along the High Line, spaces where the mood of the
park seems to change over the course of just a
block or two. In the southern half these places are
signaled by cavernous tunnels that go through
former industrial buildings and deliver the visitor
into a new type of landscape: a sun deck or a
horticultural preserve. In the northern section is the
Chelsea Thicket, which runs between 21st and
22nd Streets. This is the densest part of the park;
walking through it, particularly when the trees
are in leaf, is like entering a passageway to a secret
kingdom. When you come from the south you
emerge onto the High Line's much-loved lawn; if
you pass through from the north you end up in
the Chelsea Grasslands, an open, sun-filled expanse.
Either way, the forest of the Chelsea Thicket,
with its mix of evergreens and deciduous trees,
encloses you, giving you the unique sensation of
being — if just for a moment — in the woods.

Lost Graffiti of the High Line

Before the High Line was completed there was enough graffiti on adjacent buildings to fill a Chelsea art gallery. But call it what you will, the City of New York considers it all — rollers, "fill-ins," tags, or "throw-ups" — a sign of urban decay. In the months leading up to the park's 2009 grand opening the Graffiti Free NYC truck rolled into the neighborhood and removed much of the art, or blight, that had accumulated over the decades. Some tags survived, and new ones pop up regularly.

Installation view of *ACT UP New York: Activism, Art, and the AIDS Crisis*, 1987–1993, at White Columns in 2010. Courtesy White Columns, New York.

Rubin Museum of Art.
Courtesy Rubin Museum of Art, New York.

MUSEUM MILE-AND-A-HALF

The neighborhood the High Line cuts through is transforming into the most important concentration of contemporary art in the United States. Twenty-five years ago pioneering arts organizations began moving north from SoHo, attracted by affordable real estate prices and the more open, former industrial spaces available in Chelsea.

First to arrive was The Kitchen (*p.142*), which moved to 19th Street in 1985. Two years later the Dia Art Foundation (*p.143*) established itself on 22nd Street. Both groups chose locations that were just steps from the High Line. A number of smaller but important arts organizations soon followed including White Columns, New York's oldest alternative art space, which was founded in 1970 and moved to Chelsea in 1998. White Columns has showcased the early work of William Wegman, Sarah Sze, David Wojnarowicz, Glenn Ligon, and Sonic Youth.

In 2001, Printed Matter (*p.144*), which was founded in 1976 in Tribeca, moved from SoHo to Chelsea, followed four years later by Aperture, the foundation created in 1952 by Ansel Adams, Dorothea Lange, and Minor White to promote photographers and photography. As well as offering shows in their gallery space, Aperture continues to publish its quarterly magazine and high-quality books. A bit north, in Hell's Kitchen, is Exit Art, an interdisciplinary cultural center with an activist edge; it presents exhibitions, films, and performances that confront issues of race, ethnicity, gender, sexuality, politics, and the environment.

Both Dia and the Whitney Museum of American Art (*p.54*) are creating significant new spaces near the High Line, and the number of commercial art galleries in the neighborhood has doubled in ten years. Specialty museums have moved in as well, including the Rubin, dedicated to the art of the Himalayas. And Friends of the High Line presents site-specific artwork throughout the year, both in and around the park. With its extraordinary collection of exhibition and performance spaces, this neighborhood is fast becoming Downtown's Museum Mile-and-a-Half, a modern counterpart to the Upper East Side's famous Museum Mile.

THE GALLERY SCENE

Chelsea has become a magnet for art galleries. In the 1990s a wave of commercial gallery owners from overcrowded SoHo began moving here, beginning with Matthew Marks, who opened at 522 West 22nd Street in 1994. Paula Cooper, who had opened the first gallery in SoHo in 1968, followed two years later. At the time an art writer described Chelsea to *New York* magazine as "Blade Runner on the Hudson. . . . Even the cops are scared to go there." Today there are more than 350 art galleries from 16th to 27th Streets and between Tenth and Eleventh Avenues — so many that some building owners have been forced to post notices on their front doors that say "Private Residence" or "This is not a gallery!"

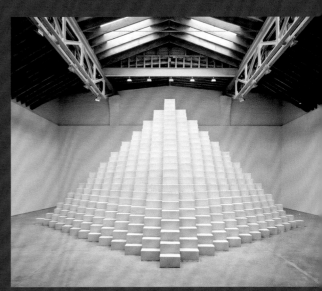

Sol LeWitt, *Four-Sided Pyramid*, 1997, concrete blocks (approximately 1100) and mortar, 180⅜ x 398½ x 382¼ in. © 2011 The LeWitt Estate / Artists Rights Society (ARS), New York. Courtesy Paula Cooper Gallery, New York. Photo Tom Powel.

David Byrne, *Tight Spot*, view of installation underneath the High Line at The Pace Gallery, New York City, 2011. Cold air inflatable with audio, 20 x 48 x 48 ft. © David Byrne. Courtesy The Pace Gallery, New York. Photo Scott Mlyn.

David Byrne and the Talking Heads, *Live at The Kitchen*, 1976.
Photo ©Kathy Landman, courtesy The Kitchen.

Alix Pearlstein, *After the Fall*, 2008 (installation).
Photo ©David B. Smith, courtesy The Kitchen.

THE KITCHEN

The Kitchen was formed in 1971 as an artists'
collective, originally operating out of the kitchen
at the Mercer Arts Center in Greenwich Village.
The group later moved to its own space in SoHo,
where it presented not only established artists
such as John Cage but also helped launch the
careers of many new names in art, dance, and music:
Laurie Anderson, Eric Bogosian, Philip Glass, Bill T.
Jones/Arnie Zane, Miranda July, Sherrie Levine,
Meredith Monk, Steve Reich, Cindy Sherman, and
even the Beastie Boys. David Byrne and the Talking
Heads made early appearances there. In 1985, The
Kitchen purchased a handsome former ice factory
at 512 West 19th, where it created an expansive
performance space for artists exploring new
ideas in dance, music, literature, video, and film.

Jay Scheib, *Bellona, Destroyer of Cities*, 2010.
Photo ©Julieta Cervantes, courtesy The Kitchen.

Sarah Michelson, *Devotion*, 2011. Photo ©Paula Court, courtesy The Kitchen.

Dan Graham, *Two-Way Mirror Cylinder Inside Cube*, 1981/1991, and Video Lounge. From "Rooftop Urban Park Project," Dia Art Foundation, 548 West 22nd Street, New York. September 12, 1991–94. Courtesy Dia Art Foundation, New York. Photo Bill Jacobson.

Robert Gober, site-specific installation at Dia Art Foundation, 548 West 22nd Street, New York. September 24, 1992–June 20, 1993. Courtesy Dia Art Foundation, New York. Photo Bill Jacobson.

DIA:CHELSEA

Dia Art Foundation was founded in the early 1970s to support artists whose work often exceeded the conventions of standard museum spaces. In fact the name "Dia" was taken from the Greek word meaning "through," and was chosen to suggest the institution's role in enabling visionary artistic projects that otherwise might not be realized because of their scale or ambition. When Dia opened a space in Chelsea in 1987, it offered entire floors to artists including Robert Gober, Jenny Holzer, Roni Horn, Brice Marden, and Richard Serra, and committed to in-depth, long-term exhibitions that would extend for a much longer period of time than other institutions, from ten months to a full year.

Dia:Chelsea is just one part of the expansive Dia Art Foundation. Dia:Beacon houses the organization's permanent collection of major works from the 1960s to the present and is located in a former Nabisco factory seventy miles north on the Hudson River. Dia also maintains and operates site-specific projects on Long Island and in the American West.

[2,3]

TAUBA AUERBACH

Printed Matter, 195 Tenth Avenue, New York. Photo Scott Mlyn.

PRINTED MATTER

In addition to being a thriving center for galleries and arts organizations, Chelsea is also home to a great many writers. On opposite sides of Tenth Avenue between 21st and 22nd Streets are two storefronts that embrace every manifestation of the printed word. On the west side is Printed Matter, the world's largest nonprofit organization dedicated to publications conceived by artists. Along with a public reading room that holds approximately 15,000 books, it also hosts an active educational series, runs an acclaimed publishing program, has an online Research Room with a comprehensive bibliographic database for scholars, and puts on the annual New York Art Book Fair for collectors, publishers, antiquarian dealers, and other art enthusiasts. Directly across the street is the highly regarded independent bookstore 192 Books. Often described as feeling more like a private library than a bookstore, it offers a carefully chosen list of titles in literature, history, memoir, science, and children's books. Like its neighbor across the street, the store is a fixture in the community and hosts an ongoing series of readings and author events. It also presents the occasional art exhibit

CHURCH OF THE GUARDIAN ANGEL

The Church of the Guardian Angel, with its red-tiled roof, stands on 21st Street and Tenth Avenue. Founded in 1888, the Catholic parish was originally located on 23rd Street; it had to move when the elevated railroad — today's High Line — was built. On school days, in sun, rain, or snow, the crossing guard is a giveaway that there are young students here too; they attend the parish school that opened in 1931, the year the Church moved to its new location on land that had been transferred to it by the New York Central Railroad. The stained-glass windows visitors pass by on the High Line depict an anchor, a heart, and a lily, which signify faith, hope, and charity.

HOLLY ON THE HIGH LINE

The classic American holly tree, *Ilex opaca*, set in a grove near the Chelsea Thicket, is the species most associated with Christmas, and is often referred to as "Christmas holly." It's well situated in this part of Chelsea, former farmland developed by Clement Clarke Moore, who wrote the famous poem about St. Nicholas that concludes: "Happy Christmas to all, and to all a good-night" (*p.121*). In winter the American holly has bright red berries that are poisonous to humans but immensely attractive to songbirds and many kinds of mammals. The wood of the tree is often used for detail work by cabinetmakers. Another holly known as winterberry, *Ilex verticillata* 'Winter Red,' can be found in the Gansevoort Woodland. It, like American holly, requires both a male and female plant in order to pollinate. The male that accompanies the female winterberry is 'Southern Gentleman.' The gallantly named 'Jersey Knight' assists the female American holly, which is known, oddly enough, as 'Dan Fenton.'

20th–23rd Streets

HL23

The metallic, curving building at 23rd Street and Tenth Avenue is (somewhat pretentiously) known as HL23, which makes it the first, but by no means the last, piece of architecture to be named after the park. It was designed by Los Angeles architect Neil Denari, and it's a rare building in that it gets wider — by as much as forty percent — as it rises above its much smaller street-level footprint. This design, the result of New York's strict zoning laws, allows it to lean over its namesake. As the architecture critic for the *Los Angeles Times* put it: "HL23 behaves like a flower planted along the park's underside that manages to grow up and out over its urban host."

SPEARS BUILDING AND SEATING STEPS

The Spears Building was constructed in 1888 by the Kinney Tobacco Company, part of the giant American Tobacco Company which, until it was broken up by antitrust laws, controlled more than ninety percent of the American tobacco market. In 1892 a five-alarm fire gutted the entire factory and reportedly destroyed forty million cigarettes. The headline in the *New York Times* announced: "One Fiend Beats Another." In 1931 the eastern part of the factory was demolished to make way for the High Line; the windows behind the seating steps are the former loading docks that connected the factory to the railroad.

Having observed people in the park's first section, the designers of the High Line knew that visitors "like to linger"; so in the second half they created more and varied seating opportunities. The amphitheater-style seats that abut the Spears Building were an attempt to provide "a big exhibitionist space" that would create a unique spot for people-watching and, in the words of landscape architect James Corner, "actually theatricalize the relationship between the viewer and the viewed."

Faded but still visible on the brick wall above it all is the signature of the famous duo REVS COST (the anonymous Revs and his partner Adam Cost), who painted graffiti tags all over New York City during the 1990s (*pp.18, 138*).

20th–22rd Streets

At the core of our love of lawns is the fact that we humans, like every other animal ever studied, possess an innate habitat preference — a built-in attraction to and comfort with a particular landscape that equates with safety and survival.

— John Falk

THE LAWN

John Falk, a professor at Oregon State University who has spent more than four decades studying the relationship of people and lawns, observes that humans "were born to the lawn." For millions of years, he writes, "hundreds of thousands of generations of our early human ancestors lived out their lives on the short grass, the lawn-like savannas of Africa, environments that looked amazingly like modern-day urban parks. In other words, there really was a Garden of Eden, and although most of

us no longer live on the savannas of Africa, each of us still carries the genetic 'memory' of that paradise within us."

The High Line's lawn instantly became one of the most popular places in the park when it opened in spring 2011. At 4,900 square feet, it's just a patch, really — a far cry from Sheep's Meadow in Central Park, Manhattan's Great Lawn — and it closes frequently "for restoration." But it's a lawn in the sky; and day and night it beckons, offering people of all ages a place to romp or read, doze, kiss, have a picnic, or simply sit, watch, and listen.

Yes, there might well be a place for a small lawn in my new garden.
— Michael Pollan, *Second Nature: A Gardener's Education*

Michael Pollan, in *Second Nature,* wrestles with the concept of the lawn in American life: its primal allure as a place of safety for humans and grazing for animals, against the demands it makes on us to both subdue and perfect it. Gardening, he writes, "tutors us in nature's ways, fostering an ethic of give-and-take with respect to the land." Lawns, on the other hand, require that we dominate nature, take "a knife" to the land, "bend nature to our will." Toward the end of the argument he has with himself about what place a lawn might deserve in his garden, the analogy turns writerly.

"If lawn mowing feels like copying the same sentence over and over, gardening is like writing out new ones, an infinitely variable process of invention and discovery."

The High Line park, with its exquisite mix of plants, varied horticultural landscapes, and, yes, small lawn, has become the perfect place to enjoy and contemplate this human conundrum — even when the lawn is closed for restoration.

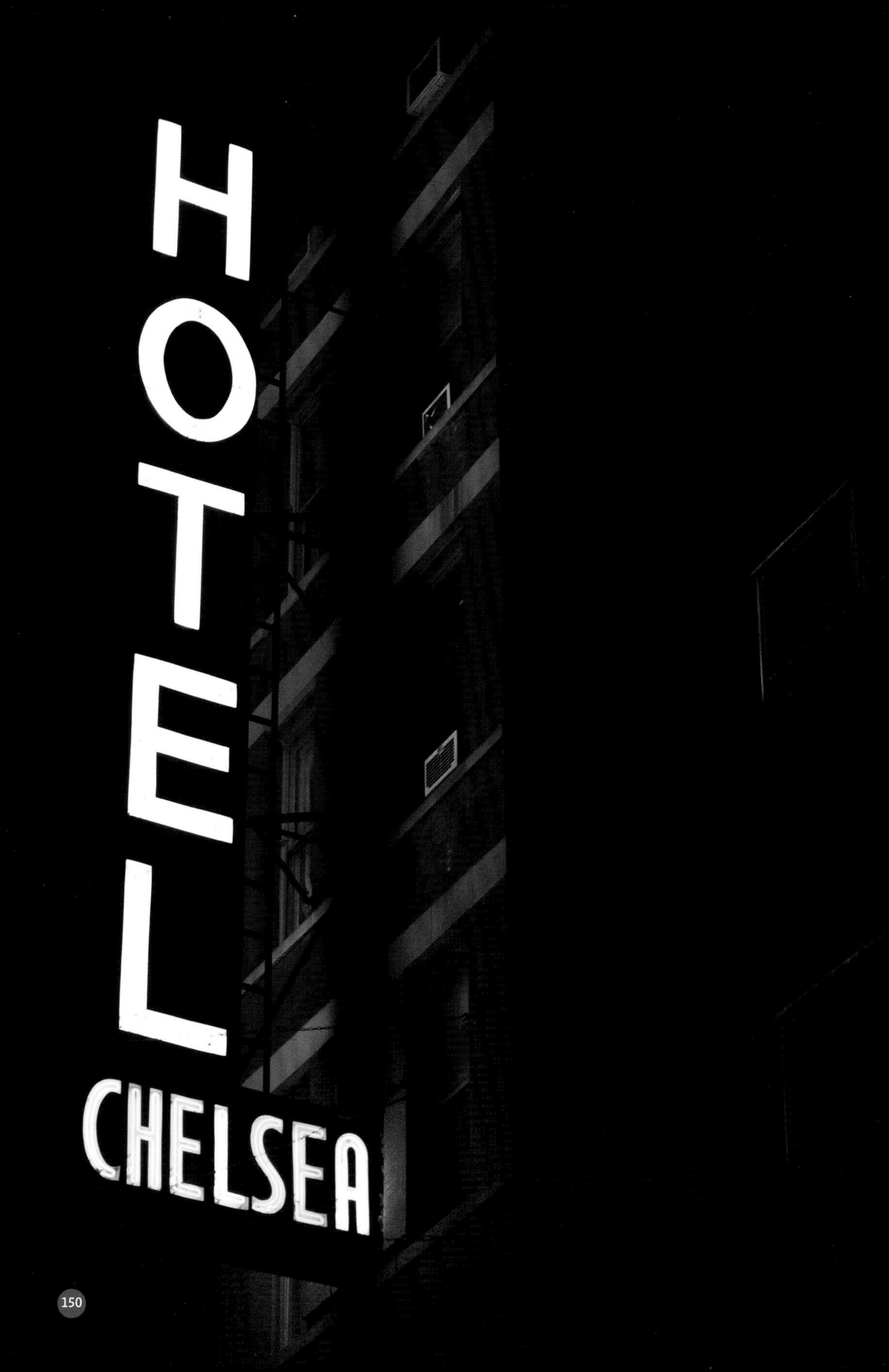
HOTEL
CHELSEA

John Baeder, *EMPIRE DINER*, 1999, oil on canvas, 30 x 48 in., The Seavest Collection of Contemporary Realism. Photo T. Adam Woods.

THE CHELSEA HOTEL

Chelsea was one of New York's original bohemias and has long been home to writers, musicians, actors, photographers, filmmakers, and artists. Many lived or stayed at the famous Chelsea Hotel, whose sign on the south side of 23rd Street is visible from the High Line. It opened in 1884 as one of New York's first co-op apartment buildings and became a hotel twenty years later. The place is, as one reporter described it, "thick with spirits." Mark Twain lived there — at the time it was the tallest building in New York — as did Simone de Beauvoir, Jane Fonda, Dennis Hopper, Arthur Miller, Jean-Paul Sartre, Elaine Stritch, Dylan Thomas, Yevgeni Yevtushenko, Tennessee Williams, and countless others. Many great works were created at the Chelsea Hotel: Arthur C. Clark's *2001: A Space Odyssey*, Jack Kerouac's *On the Road*, William S. Burroughs' *Naked Lunch*, and Virgil Thomson's first American opera, *Lord Byron*. Andy Warhol filmed *The Chelsea Girls* there, and Leonard Cohen immortalized it in song ("I remember you well in the Chelsea Hotel").

THE EMPIRE DINER

Joining the trend of naming new buildings and commercial enterprises after the popular park is the The Highliner, recently reopened in 2011 after decades as the Empire Diner. Built by the Fodero Dining Car Company in 1946, the place was first called Arthur's Diner, but it remained a greasy spoon until the 1970s when it was remodeled by new owners, launching a trend of retro diners across the country. West Chelsea was grungy and dangerous in those days, but the Empire Diner attracted a stream of celebrities along with drag queens, actors, and musicians who would drop by to play an upright piano in the back. The diner has appeared in many movies, including *Men in Black* and Woody Allen's *Manhattan,* as well as on various television programs. A photo of the now-landmarked Empire Diner in the famous opening credits of *Saturday Night Live* has guaranteed its place in popular culture.

The Warehouse Law

New Amsterdam, later Manhattan, began as an entrepreneurial venture to enable trade — primarily in beaver pelts — by the Dutch West India Company. Reports of its earliest days include mention of warehouses "for storing furs and transferring them to ships." The book *Dutch New York* describes the active commercial waterfront of 1664 as "rows of closely built brick, stepped, or spout-gabled townhouses and warehouses." Since the Industrial Revolution warehouses have been an essential part of West Chelsea, fueled by two key factors: the explosion of foreign and domestic trade on the Hudson River waterfront and passage of the Warehousing Act of 1846, which allowed private companies to warehouse goods and defer the payment of fees or taxes until products had been reshipped or picked up by the consignee. Defending that law twenty-five years later, the Storekeeper of the Port of New York noted that England's similar arrangement "made her the mistress of the commerce of the world," a position New Yorkers have vied for since the days of Henry Hudson.

All along the High Line one can see the modern equivalent of the 17th-century Dutch storehouse, led by the ubiquitous Manhattan Mini Storage and its humorous billboard advertising. The three brick buildings on 20th Street just west of the High Line and directly across from the Kingdom Hall of Jehovah's Witnesses once belonged to the Baker & Williams Company, which operated "bonded," or duty-free, warehouses around the city as a direct benefit of the 1846 law. It's also the site that helps explain how the Manhattan Project got its name. In the 1940s this set of buildings was used as a top-secret government facility for storing tons of processed uranium, which was being studied as part of the research effort that led to the production of the atom bomb. This was one of at least ten locations in Manhattan that participated in the atomic energy project, and it is the only facility still in existence. Today it houses galleries and related businesses. Friends of the High Line has its offices next door in No. 529.

View of Pike's Opera House at corner of Eighth Avenue and 23rd Street, New York. Image by Rockwood, 1868.

CENTER OF AMUSEMENTS

In the 1870s and 1880s, Chelsea was the heart of New York's theater district. Or, as *The WPA Guide to New York City* described it, "center of amusements." Most prominent was Pike's Opera House, later renamed the Grand Opera House, on Eighth Avenue and 23rd Street, which seated 2,000 people, provided standing room for 1,500 more, and had one of the largest stages in New York. Dozens of theaters in the neighborhood put on a full array of productions: drama, comedy, farce, melodrama, spectacle, "sensational plays," ballet, Italian opera, and vaudeville.

In 1912, Adolph Zukor founded the Famous Players Film Company and pioneered a new theatrical art form in Chelsea: the motion picture. The company's first release featured Sarah Bernhardt; over the years other stars, many from the stage, became Famous Players, including John Barrymore and Mary Pickford. In the 1950s Zukor's building, a former armory for the Ninth Mounted Cavalry, was renamed Chelsea Studios; since then it has been used for both movies and television shows, including *BUtterfield 8*, *Twelve Angry Men*, *The French Connection*, both incarnations of Mel Brooks's classic comedy *The Producers*, and episodes of *The Patty Duke Show*, *The Honeymooners,* and *Guiding Light*.

THE RIVER THAT DOESN'T RUN THROUGH IT

Before the Civil War the Hudson River flowed below where the modern High Line now stands. In his 1854 *Autobiography* the Rev. Samuel H. Turner, a professor at General Theological Seminary, describes how, in the 1820s, "The Hudson River at high tide washed what is now the Tenth Avenue," and how the mud was frequently so deep "as to make it inaccessible, except on horseback or in a carriage." In the 19th century the city began selling "water lots," and developers rushed in to buy up chunks of the Hudson River, which they filled in and developed into factories, warehouses, and living quarters for the surging immigrant population that was flooding New York. Over the centuries landfill has been used to extend Manhattan Island in various areas, including in Battery Park City, which was built in the 1990s on soil and rock excavated during construction of the World Trade Center. But even as the City giveth, the City taketh away: Thirteenth Avenue, built on landfill in the 1830s, was later destroyed to create a new port that could accommodate huge luxury ocean liners like the *Titanic* and the *Lusitania* (pp.43, 113). Today everything east of the Hudson River to around Tenth Avenue and running north from Horatio to 23rd Streets is built on landfill.

PUBLISHING AND PRINTING

New York has a long, illustrious history as a center of printing and the publishing trades. In 1913 a trade group boasted that "As early as 1693 New York City showed its progressive spirit by offering fifty pounds a year to any printer who would start a plant within the city." By the second decade of the 20th century the *New York Times* declared that Chelsea was rapidly becoming the new center of that industry. The former factory of the H. Wolff Book Manufacturing Company (*p.165*) is on 26th Street, and the faded lettering of the American Book Bindery Building and the Stratford Press can be seen a bit farther north. The *New York Daily News* and Associated Press are both headquartered in the Westyard Distribution Center, the oddly shaped, monolithic brown building on 33rd Street that is a noted example of the style of Brutalism in architecture (*below*). Throughout its history Chelsea has also been an important center for photography. In the 1880s the New York Photogravure Company — which a popular contemporary guidebook called "a monument of artistic New York" — was based on 23rd Street. Today there are dozens of photography studios, labs, graphic design firms, and camera stores throughout Chelsea.

London Terrace Apartments

The London Terrace apartment complex was built on land originally purchased by Captain Thomas Clarke in 1750, when the entire area was farmland owned by an old Dutch family called Somerindyck. Clarke named his estate Chelsea after a hospital in London where old soldiers went to live upon leaving the army. His grandson, Clement Clarke Moore, developed the property in the 19th century and kept the British theme alive by calling it London Terrace, building a series of elegant brownstones on 23rd Street that came to be known as "Millionaires' Row."

Henry Mandel, often described as "the Donald Trump of the 1920s," demolished eighty old houses to build today's London Terrace Towers, which occupies the full block between 23rd and 24th Streets bounded by Ninth and Tenth Avenues. When it opened in 1930 it was the largest, most luxurious apartment building in the world. A promotional film promised future residents "a kingdom all your own" with a beautiful indoor swimming pool, an acre of gardens, a gymnasium, a nursery, a penthouse club for adults, and a sun terrace "exclusively for the babies." A roof deck was fitted out with steamer chairs that offered "a true sea setting" with views of luxury ocean liners in their berths at the Chelsea Piers. Uniformed page boys delivered messages and packages to tenants, and the building even had its own newsletter, the *Tatler*. But the most famous feature was the doorman's uniform, modeled on the attire of the London policeman, the Bobby, helmet and all. For the first few years that London Terrace was open there was a daily changing of the guard — announced by bugle — at 4:45 p.m.

Henry Mandel began his project in the late 1920s, but by 1934 the Great Depression had ruined him. Although urban legend has it that he then jumped to his death from the roof of his own building, Mandel, while he did go bankrupt, died quietly in a hospital in 1942. The building's stately and distinctive brick water towers with their arched windows and crenellated moldings can be seen from various points along the High Line.

Other High Lines – *by Rick Darke*

In railroad parlance, a high line is an elevated track. They're most often called elevateds, El's, or viaducts, terms that overlap with high line. For example, the West Philadelphia Elevated is also known as the High Line. Many high lines are simply tracks running over raised ground. Others, such as Philadephia's Reading Viaduct, ride on steel, stone, and concrete or, like New York's High Line, on all-steel structures. Each is essentially a bridge. Originally built to cross city streets, uneven ground, or waterways, an increasing number are finding new life as bridges between urban communities and their local ecologies.

Bridge of Flowers, *Shelburne Falls, Massachusetts*
New York's High Line may be the most spectacular park made from an old railway but it is not the first. That honor belongs to the Bridge of Flowers. Built in 1908 as a trolley bridge, it extends 400 feet on concrete arches over the Deerfield River. After the railway went bankrupt in 1927, the Shelburne Falls Women's Club transformed the abandoned bridge into a linear garden, open to visitors since 1929.

Reading Viaduct, *Philadelphia*
Of the many railway-to-park projects in progress, the Reading Viaduct bears the closest relation to the High Line. Completed in 1893 by the Philadelphia and Reading Railroad to bring passengers to the new Reading Terminal, it carried countless trains on four tracks until 1981. Though now truncated at the south end, three-quarters of a mile of the abandoned elevated 9th Street Branch remains and, in High Line fashion, has become a wild garden. Unlike the High Line, the Viaduct was electrified in 1929. The latticed catenary bridges that once supported charged copper wires are a highly sculptural presence. Though it has long been the dream of a few community groups to conserve the Viaduct as walkable open space, these efforts have been galvanized by the High Line's success. Design visions with a lower cost and maintenance approach that celebrate the ecological and economic efficiencies of ruderal landscapes are gaining traction.

Promenade Plantée, *12th Arr., Paris, France*
Built on a former railroad right-of-way which from 1859 to 1969 carried trains from Gare de la Bastille to Paris's eastern suburbs, the Promenade Plantée provided direct inspiration for the High Line. At its 1920s' peak the elegant station served more than 30,000,000 passengers annually, yet by 1969 a new high-speed métro had made it obsolete. The

station was demolished in 1984; however the brick and stone viaduct extending from it along avenue Daumesnil survived. After a period of abandonment, the trackway atop the viaduct was refashioned into the world's first elevated park, opening in 1989. Construction of extended pedestrian paths at and below grade continued until 1994, bringing the length to two and a half miles. Plantings are formal, relying on clipped trees and shrubs that often separate visitors from views of the city. In this way the Promenade is unlike the High Line. Spaces under the viaduct's seventy arches have been converted into arcades housing studios and workshops for nearly fifty artisans, interspersed with restaurants and cafes. Known as the Viaduc des Arts, it is eloquent proof of the new roles old railways can play in today's cities.

ON THE HIGH LINE

23RD–26TH STREETS

THE SLOW PARK

Visitors to the High Line find themselves oddly, ineluctably, slowed by the park. The normal, frenetic pace of Manhattan doesn't seem to exist here. Even in the rain — even in a storm — people move slowly. Perhaps it's the pull of old and new that slows our pace: the monumentality of aging industrial buildings set against showy pieces of modern architecture. An age-old form of transportation with its rusty rail ties hovers above a 21st-century alternative: a motorized scooter drifts by on one side, a Tesla electric car is parked on the other. The meadow at 24th Street is a bridge between two canyons, with shiny new buildings at the southern end and industrial smokestacks at the northern. It's one of those wonderful transitional areas on the High Line that defies a visitor to feel stress or the need for haste. The grasses and flowers bend in the wind, as if on a prairie, and in summer blast their color and scent across the park and into the streets below.

TREE OF HEAVEN: FROM BELOVED TO BEMOANED

Ailanthus altissima, tree of heaven, was introduced to America in 1784 by a plant collector who fell victim to the "chinoiserie" craze then sweeping England and France. By the 19th century this ancient Chinese tree was widely planted along public walks in America's leading cities. *Ailanthus* grows quickly, in sparse soil and punishing weather conditions, and it grows high, providing abundant shade. The male is a particularly tough urban character: it elicits a smell so foul, insects avoid it like the plague. It was the perfect city tree, but most important, it was exotic. Andrew Jackson Downing, an early enthusiast, wrote that tree of heaven could "whisper tales to you in the evening of the 'Flowery Country' from whence you have borrowed it."

In 1943 Betty Smith forever memorialized it in her bestselling novel *A Tree Grows in Brooklyn.* She also made it instantly recognizable by insisting that her publisher illustrate the cover with a real *Ailanthus altissima.* Smith's book captures the gritty character of a tree that "grows on neglect" and fights to survive in a concrete patch; it comes to stand as a metaphor for one family's ability to overcome adversity.

But Smith also knew the once-popular tree had fallen into disfavor. In her preface she observed: "It would be considered beautiful except that there are too many of it." Even Downing eventually turned against the tree, calling it a "usurper . . . which has come over to this land of liberty, under the garb of utility, to make foul the air with its pestilent breath, and devour the soil with its intermeddling roots." By 2000, when Joel Sternfeld came to Manhattan's derelict railroad to photograph the area now known as the Flyover, tree of heaven was universally reviled as an invasive and noxious weed. But here on the High Line it found a quiet home and thrived for decades in the concrete railbed.

Joel Sternfeld, *Ailanthus Trees, 25th Street, May 2000*
Image © Joel Sternfeld. Courtesy the artist and Luhring Augustine, New York

THE FLYOVER

One of the marquee features of the High Line's northern section is the "Woodland Flyover," a steel catwalk rising eight feet above the floor of the old railbed and extending from 25th to 27th Streets. When it first opened, in spring 2011, the magnolia trees hadn't grown high enough to create the canopy that the gardeners hope will develop here in the coming years. Underneath the Flyover, High Line crews planted more than 8,000 perennials, grasses, and mosses that over time will form a dense, lush groundcover beneath the walkway. The two large buildings the Flyover passes through — the former warehouse of the R. C. Williams wholesale grocer and the H. Wolff Book Manufacturing Company — created a microclimate and sheltered the plants that grew here.

It doesn't take an architecture student to understand why this part of the park — a rather dark, narrow passage through two monolithic industrial buildings — needed a dramatic flourish that would engage visitors as they pass through. The large brick smokestack attached to 511 West 25th Street, a former tinfoil factory, is a feature that was common around New York during the Industrial Revolution and calls to mind the industrial past of the neighborhood. For people familiar with the High Line and its history, it also recalls the now-iconic photograph taken by Joel Sternfeld of the red brick smokestack at the eastern end of the old viaduct on 30th Street, with the Empire State Building in the background.

There is something very fine about a great gray mass of building, all one color, all one tone, yet modified by the sunlight or shadow to pearly gray or wonderful delicacy. It is the big simplicity of the thing that counts.

— Architect Cass Gilbert

R. C. WILLIAMS BUILDING

Backing up to the High Line at 25th–26th Streets is the former warehouse of the R.C. Williams Company, a wholesale grocer founded in 1809; by the early 20th century it had grown into a major international corporation. Designed by American architect Cass Gilbert, the warehouse was configured to take advantage of the new elevated railroad and create a highly efficient, seamless flow of goods from the boxcar, through the ware-house, and into the delivery trucks that waited on the street below. The Williams Company received the first delivery ever made on the High Line on August 1, 1933, and over the years a surprising variety of items passed through these walls, destined for the fifty states and beyond. To Russia went carpet sweepers and silverware; canned corn on the cob and shrimp went to ranchers in Argentina. Sauerkraut went to South Africa, powdered sugar to Peru. Canned oysters and brown bread went to the Netherlands, maple sugar and table salt to Germany, and pimentos, whiskey, and canned sweet potatoes to Greece. Today, the former warehouse is the flagship campus for the Avenues School (p.165).

HIGH SCHOOLS OF THE FUTURE

The neighborhood around the High Line is home to several cutting-edge high schools. On West 18th Street, in one of New York's oldest neighborhoods, is the Hudson High School of Learning Technologies, a new breed of public school where there are no textbooks and all learning is done via digital-only content. Students work on laptops and take both a real-world and an online class for each subject. Teachers post schedules, lesson plans, and curriculum archives on a website. The principal, a former Wall Street commodities trader, runs the school as part of a pilot program sponsored by the New York City Department of Education. A bit farther north, in the former R. C. Williams Company warehouse on 25th Street, is the home of the brand new Avenues World School, founded as a for-profit venture by Chris Whittle of Edison Schools and Benno C. Schmidt, the former president of Yale University. The school advertises that it will provide a global education, including courses on social entrepreneurism and world population trends. *Business Week* commented that "its plan captures the zeitgeist so well it could have been scripted by Aaron Sorkin."

H. WOLFF BOOK MANUFACTURING CO.

The H. Wolff Book Manufacturing Company, which provided printing, binding, and distribution services to publishers, had both a printing plant and a bindery annex on 26th Street. Wolff, which had no direct access to the High Line, made an agreement with its neighbor, the wholesale grocer, to transport goods via the R. C. Williams Company's rail siding. All the materials necessary for book manufacturing — paper, binding cloth, glue — arrived by truck at the Wolff factory's loading dock on 26th Street, and then finished books emerged on the High Line for distribution by train around the country.

West Chelsea was the hub of the printing business during the early 19th century. The Zinn Building at 210 Eleventh Avenue, between 24th and 25th Streets, was originally owned by a firm that made "fancy metal goods," but it leased much of its space to lithographers and printers. Farther north, on 34th and Tenth Avenue, is the Master Printers Building, which, in 1924, was the biggest commercial building west of Sixth Avenue. It was designed to be a center for the printing trades, a place where a person could find, under one roof, samples of every type of paper, inks, and machinery used in printing and lithography for books, pamphlets, and magazines.

*So atop the city that taught the world what modern cities ought to be,
there they are, the hoops and staves of the Middle Ages.*

— Charles Kuralt

WATER TOWERS

The newsman Charles Kuralt was a big admirer of the water towers that grace so many of New York's rooftops. The city requires that every building above a certain height — around six stories — must have them, both to regulate water pressure throughout the building and to help firefighters by providing a reliable source of water. To this day Manhattan's water tanks, which hold between 5,000 and 10,000 gallons each, are hand-crafted from wood and iron by one of two companies that have been making them here for more than a century. Wallace Rosenwach was one of those coopers; his grandfather started the business in 1896. While walking around the city one day with Kuralt, Wallace looked up and said: "That's our skyline. We helped create it."

The High Line is bookended by two former industrial buildings, each of which has a prominent water tower standing tall on its roof. At the southern end, on Gansevoort Street, is the former Manhattan Refrigerating Company, now the West Coast apartment building (*p.58*). At the northern end is a large, brick former furniture factory that stands across the West Side Rail Yards at 34th Street and is now the corporate headquarters of Coach leatherware. All along the High Line's path through the Meatpacking District and Chelsea, countless water towers can be seen and admired. Some are old, some are new. Most rest on a simple metal frame but some — like the ones on the London Terrace apartment building (*top left*) — have been given a place in the architecture. One pair, which sits atop an old tinfoil factory, looks like a couple of spaceships (*below, center*). Another sits alone on the remains of a brick parapet, like an ancient ruin (*below, right*). Water towers are a quintessential element of the skyline, a sure sign to a New Yorker that he's home.

WINDOWS ON WINDOWS

There are scores of windows along the High Line:
old and new, sleek and industrial, some with broken
glass, some with colored. Some — in Frank Gehry's
IAC Building (*p.168 top*) — even seem to bend
into curves, while others cut sharp angles against
a building's façade. There are empty frames that
provide a view to other windows in the distance —
windows on windows. At the Starrett-Lehigh
Building, on 26th Street, eight miles of windows
wrap around the nineteen-story former factory-
warehouse (*bottom right*).

A Park Outside My Window

Walking through the northern half of the
High Line can be an odd experience. South of
23rd Street a visitor admires the buildings
and architecture from a respectful distance, as
though passing through some great outdoor
gallery. But farther north the park passes close
by, and sometimes directly underneath, the
windows of people's homes, putting countless
details of domestic life on view. Someone's
bottle collection sits in the window, above a
flower box. A gay pride flag sits next to a sticker
for the Human Rights Campaign. A stack of
books teeters on a windowsill, and a shower
curtain betrays the location of a bathroom.
A man sneaks a cigarette on his deck while a
large hound lounges in the window.

BILLBOARD

The area around the billboard and Viewing Spur at 26th Street is one of the best places to appreciate New York's architecture from the High Line. Day or night, the group of tall spires from the Empire State, Bank of America, *New York Times,* and Condé Nast buildings frames a striking view of the cityscape (*pp.176–77*). At night the imposing sign on the New Yorker Hotel, once the largest in New York, can be seen to the north.

The large, empty billboard frame that looks down on 26th Street is there as a reference to the many advertising billboards that were attached to the High Line when it was a working railroad. Today visitors in the park can sit in an expansive wooden lounge seat and gaze through the frame to the street below. Passersby on Tenth Avenue who look up from street level get to see real people instead of advertising models.

THE MODERN LUXURY CRUISE

Long gone are the great ocean liners that used these piers in the glory days of transatlantic travel — the *Lusitania, Mauretania, Queen Elizabeth, Queen Mary, Normandie* — but the Hudson River port continues to thrive with the modern-day equivalent, operated by companies like Carnival, Princess, and Norwegian Cruise Lines. When the Art Deco–inspired *Ile de France* sailed into New York Harbor in 1927 its marble and gold dining room with chrome fountain in the center was the talk of the town. The ship's chapel had fourteen pillars and was designed in the Gothic style; for entertainment there was a shooting gallery (for adults) and a merry-go-round (for children). The huge "Fun Ships" of today also cater to the whole family, but the main attractions include adult-only retreats that promise

"me-time," 18-hole mini-golf, video arcades, jumbo movie screens, and water slides.

There are many places along the High Line from which to watch a cruise ship pass by, and if you close your eyes as the captain signals the deep, bellowing blast of the ship's horn you can almost picture the glorious *Ile de France* gliding into her berth at the Chelsea Piers. *Almost.*

OTIS ELEVATOR COMPANY

Founded in 1853, the Otis Elevator Company has a long history of innovation, beginning with a safety feature on the mechanical hoist that prevented an elevator's platform from falling if the lifting rope was severed. In the 19th century, Otis perfected the hydraulic and electric-powered elevator. In the 20th century it invented "people movers." By the

21st century it had developed a system to transport vehicles to the 94th floor of an exhibition hall in China. The company's headquarters, at 260 Eleventh Avenue, between 26th and 27th Streets, was built on land formerly occupied by one of the many sawmills that existed in this part of West Chelsea during the mid-19th century; it housed elegant offices as well as a machine shop and forge.

If the history of skyscrapers in America is the dramatic story of a race to the top, the Otis Elevator Company played a leading role. It installed elevators in several buildings that became the world's tallest, including the Woolworth Building (1910–13), Empire State Building (1930–31), Chrysler Building (1928–30), the Twin Towers of the World Trade Center (1966–73), and the Sears Tower in Chicago (1970–73). Otis has been around long to enough to have both installed (in the 1880s) and later modernized (in 2002) the elevators in the Eiffel Tower, and it remains the world's largest manufacturer of elevators, escalators, and moving walkways.

Magnolias

Magnolias belong to one of the oldest and most primitive families of flowering plants in the world. The bigleaf magnolia is a tree that looks almost tropical: its leaves have an unusually bold visual texture that makes the tree look like it came straight from the set of Steven Spielberg's *Jurassic Park*.

The much smaller-leaved sweetbay magnolia is another North American species. It was the first magnolia to be introduced in Europe, arriving there in 1688. In some places — but certainly not here — the tree will grow as high as sixty feet, and its extremely fragrant flowers carry a lemony scent. Early settlers in North America used the bark of the sweetbay magnolia to make a tincture for treating fever, coughs, and colds.

WEST CHELSEA

West Chelsea — the area that runs roughly from
17th to 30th Streets and from Ninth Avenue to the
Hudson River — is an architecturally important
neighborhood and is also known for its mixed population. A 2005 article in the *New York Times* made
note of the neighborhood's "sometimes stunning
cheek-by-jowl incongruity." Over the decades it
has seen waves of seamen and immigrants, writers,
artists and actors, gay men (famous as "Chelsea
boys"), garment and factory workers, and, today, an
endless stream of yuppies and tourists. West
Chelsea is a classic urban neighborhood of mixed
uses that include art galleries, manufacturing and
storage facilities, parking lots, auto repair shops,
car washes, photo and film production studios,
restaurants, bars, and nightclubs. In recent years it
has become an increasingly popular residential area.
The neighborhood's former factories and ware-

23rd–26th Streets

houses had high ceilings and broad expanses of
oversized windows that reduced the need
for artificial lighting during more industrial times;
recently, many have been converted into loft
spaces, and new condominiums — some by inter-
nationally famous architects — have been built
on both sides of the High Line.

New York is one of the only states in the
country with a constitutional mandate to provide
for "the aid, care and support of the needy" through
public housing, and West Chelsea is home to two
large subsidized housing projects, both between
Ninth and Tenth Avenues: the Fulton Houses
(1965), named for engineer and inventor Robert
Fulton, on 16th to 19th Streets, and the Chelsea-
Elliott Houses (1964), named for humanist John
Lovejoy Elliott, between 25th and 26th Streets.
Between 23rd and 29th Streets and Ninth and
Tenth Avenues is Penn South, a limited-equity co-
operative apartment building for moderate-income
residents that was sponsored by the International
Ladies' Garment Workers' Union in the 1950s as
part of a national effort by the United Housing
Foundation to create good and affordable housing
at a moderate cost. Penn South was also the site of
the community board meeting where Joshua David
and Robert Hammond first met in August 1999.

New York Times

Condé Nast

Bank of America Tower

THE GREAT SPIRES

The *New York Times* headquarters on Eighth Avenue between 40th and 41st Streets was designed by Renzo Piano and completed in 2007. It was considered to be such an important piece of architecture that photographer Annie Leibovitz produced a photo-documentary of its construction, inspired by Margaret Bourke-White, who had photographed the Chrysler Building as it was being built, and Lewis W. Hine, who documented construction of the Empire State Building. The façade of the building is a curtain of ceramic rods that rises from street level to the roof; together the rods form an unending series of vertical slats that reduces energy costs by helping to block direct sunlight. The

exterior cladding also encourages climbers: at least three men have been arrested trying to summit the building. The most distinctive element that can be seen from the High Line is the 1,000-foot mast on the roof; it contains radiometers that gather and transmit solar data to a computer system that in turn controls the window shades throughout the building.

The Bank of America Tower at One Bryant Park is the first skyscraper designed to achieve a Platinum LEED rating from the U.S. Green Building Council; it was decreed the greenest building in Manhattan by the New York Academy of Sciences. Its 255-foot ornamental spire consists of 368 LED floodlights and was designed to create a performance of light that would engage

Empire State Building

Chrysler Building

23rd–26th Streets

with, and play off of, the spires of other tall skyscrapers around town, both near and far. When the lights first went on a few days after Christmas in 2010 the *New York Post* cheered that "the City That Never Sleeps has a new reason to stay up at night."

Completed in 2000, the Condé Nast building in Times Square is also considered a green building and was recognized by the American Institute of Architects for its use of solar and fuel-cell technology. Its 300-foot mast is used to support television and radio broadcasters, and at night it joins the Bank of America spire in a beautiful display of light and color.

Also visible from various points along the High Line is the Chrysler Building, an Art Deco

gem completed in 1930 when the elevated railroad that became the High Line was still in the planning stages. At that time, as Kate Ascher describes in her book *The Heights,* architects competed fiercely for the status of highest building in New York. The competition was so serious in the 1920s that "the spire of the Chrysler Building was constructed in secret and then raised into place from within the building to ensure that the tower would be able to claim the 'world's tallest title'" from a competitor downtown. For a short time it was the tallest building in the world, but in 1931 the Empire State Building — visible and always inspiring from many places along the High Line — opened for business, eclipsing it.

Like every public project in New York City the High Line has seen its share of controversy. Residents of Chelsea fought bitterly when Friends of the High Line advocated for a special tax district that would increase local property taxes. At least one new condominium development instituted an annual fee as part of its common charges, to be paid to Friends of the High Line for upkeep of the park. When the arrangement was announced the *New York Observer* responded: "What next? Will condo owners with great views of the Hudson River be assessed a sunset fee?" After the northern section opened the *New York Post* published an article headlined "Life on the 'Pry' Line" and quoted residents who were "sick of voyeurs." Complaints have come from artists too; Robert Lederman has been jailed more than once for asserting his First Amendment right to sell his artwork in the park. "They're using the High Line as if it were private property," he told a reporter.

Here are some voices from across the decades about the High Line:

The elevated highway has become familiar enough nowadays to be accepted without wonder. The roving New Yorker gets a bigger thrill out of the New York Central's elevated freight road. Leaving the surface of Eleventh Avenue below 34th Street, the railroad is set free from the city street map and takes directions of its own. High in the air, it cuts through city blocks. It passes into big buildings on its path and emerges on the other side to continue on its way, leaping any cross streets it meets.

— L. H. Robbins, *New York Times*, June 3, 1934

The High Line is not the eighth wonder of the world, not the Hanging Gardens of Babylon, but the place where all the pigeons seem to make their nests, a huge, ugly, dirty and dangerous structure and an absolute prison wall. We want demolition of the High Line as soon as possible. We thought the only question was who will pay for it.

— Cheryl Kupper, community member who testified for the Council of Chelsea Block Associations, quoted in *The Villager*, April 25, 2001

Slightly before 2:50 a.m. the building began to quiver and shake: an unearthly shrill series of screeches, wheezings and the rattlings of Brobdingnagian chains seemed headed straight for the window by my bed. I groped for my glasses and peered out between the dusty slats of the Venetian blinds. A decrepit freight train was creeping out of the south side of the Manhattan Meat & Refrigeration Warehouse across the street. Huge refrigerated trucks were parked along Washington St., their motors running, spewing noxious fumes that were already seeping through my closed windows. Then the raw steer carcasses started to roll and the odor of blood and hacked-apart flesh mixed with the other charming aromas. The High Line was making its deliveries . . .

— Patricia Fieldsteel, recalling the 1970s High Line, *The Villager*, April 2, 2003

Ms. [Judith] Courtney can't shake the fantasy that she always saw the trains disappearing into the buildings — but never coming out. "I think they went into an alternate universe, like Harry Potter."

— Meera Subramanian, *New York Times*, February 5, 2005

22nd–26th Streets

Heavy Metal in West Chelsea

In the 19th century the blocks between 25th and 26th Streets to the west of the High Line were mainly occupied by the foundry, pattern, and metal-fitting shops of the Cornell Iron Works, one of New York's largest producers of cast-iron architectural elements. During the Civil War, Cornell manufactured the revolving turrets of the ironclad warship monitors USS *Miantonomoh* and USS *Tonawanda*. The company provided steel and iron for the Park Row Building, which was the tallest office building in the world when it was constructed in 1898; the iron base and stairways of the Statue of Liberty; and 13,000 tons of steel for elevated railroad stations throughout Manhattan and Brooklyn. When Cornell moved its operations in 1900 it sold the land to the Conley Foil Company, a unit of American Tobacco. In its red brick factories on the north side of 25th Street, Conley manufactured the tinfoil that was used for cigarette packaging. In later years the buildings at 521–537 West 25th Street were leased to the Eskimo Pie Corporation and several paper-manufacturing companies, including Standard Paper Box. Today these buildings, like so many former factories and warehouses in West Chelsea, are occupied by art galleries and studios.

Another foundry, the John Williams Bronze & Iron Works, also operated nearby on 26th Street. Unlike Cornell and Conley this firm specialized in fine ornamental work — bronze and iron entrance doors, window grilles, lamp standards, statues, busts, medallions, fountains, sundials, stair railings, bank tellers' enclosures, mausoleum doors — and was one of the most prestigious manufacturers in the country. John Williams cast the bronze doors at the Library of Congress and bronze tablets at the New York Public Library. The company owned several buildings including a garage at 537 West 26th Street, which was used by one of New York's earliest fleets of taxi cabs in the 1910s and later as the studio of photographer Annie Leibovitz. Today it's home to the Cedar Lake Contemporary Ballet company.

Pharmacy in the Sky

Among the many beautiful plants on the High Line are a great number that have been used for centuries as trusted herbal remedies. The most widely used is *Echinacea* (*above*), which is believed to strengthen immunity to colds and flu. Native Americans used many of the plant species found here to treat a variety of afflictions.

Rattlesnake master, *Eryngium yuccifolium*, was used as an antidote against rattlesnake venom. Wild quinine, *Parthenium integrifolium*, and pearly everlasting, *Anaphalis margaritacea*, were used as a poultice for burns and to treat ailments like fatigue, infection, coughs, and sore throats. Joe-Pye weed, *Eupatorium fistulosum*, gets its name from the Native American word for fever, *jopi*, and was used as a remedy for typhoid fever. The plant's bold foliage is a magnet for butterflies, and its big, fluffy, lavender flower heads are striking long after the other flowers have faded for the season, staying beautiful deep into December and January. Yarrow, *Achillea filipendulina*, was named after the hero of the Trojan War, Achilles, who, according to myth, carried it to battle to treat wounds.

Plants were used for ceremonial purposes as well, including staghorn sumac, whose leaves and berries were mixed with herbs and smoked during tribal council ceremonies. People in Roman times used the perennial grassland herb purple betony, *Stachys officinalis*, to guard against sorcery, and an 11th-century herbal guide recommended it for preventing "frightful nocturnal goblins and terrible sights and dreams." It was often planted in churchyards to keep away ghosts and evil spirits.

View west past Chelsea Piers, with many railroad barges tied up alongside Pier 49 and a ship at Pier 50 being served by barges. From Robert A. Lesher, 1930, *Description of Certain Shipping Facilities in New York Harbor*, part of Complainant's Exhibit No. 152, I.C.C. Docket No. 22824 (submitted as part of a court case). Courtesy Thomas Flagg Collection.

THE TERMINAL WAREHOUSE BUILDINGS

By the middle of the 19th century New York City had become the country's center of manufacturing. In 1853 it hosted the first world's fair for the "Exhibition of the Industry of All Nations," and put on display everything from industrial machinery to fine arts. Trains were the prime movers of all these goods into and out of New York, and the many competing railroad lines faced the complex problem of freight distribution in a magnificently congested city. The solution was to build massive terminal warehouses and marshalling yards that could receive trains and unpack, store, and then reship goods of every sort, from meats to furniture.

In 1914 the Baltimore & Ohio railroad opened such a facility on Eleventh Avenue. Designed by Maurice A. Long, an engineer-architect who worked for the railroad, it's the first example of a structure built using flat-slab construction with no interior beams, which created a much larger indoor area for train tracks and warehousing. Most of the goods that passed through B&O's facility came to Manhattan via the "waterbelt" as part of the lighterage system; they were ferried over the Hudson River in boxcars from terminals on Staten Island and

New Jersey on special barges known as car floats. Phillip Lopate describes the scene in his book *Waterfront*: "So prevalent became this means of freight transport that an estimated 3,000–5,000 railroad cars floated every day across New York Harbor in the first half of the twentieth century. It is mind-boggling to think about all those flat-bottomed vessels piled high (one barge could hold eight or more carloads of freight), crossing very near each other on the crowded seas. In their heydey, the barges were almost as synonymous with New York's iconography as its skyscrapers."

Twenty years later, B&O's competitor, the Lehigh Valley Railroad, built its own terminal warehouse in partnership with the Starrett Investment Corporation. Today it's known as the Starrett-Lehigh Building, but when it opened in 1931 this 2.2-million-square-foot factory-warehouse dominated the waterfront with its huge railroad yard, loading platforms for trucks, and facilities for the storage, repacking, and distribution of goods. Today it's occupied by high-profile design, fashion, advertising, media, and publishing companies. The High Line affords many views of the enormous nineteen-story edifice and its eight miles of windows that wrap around the building (p. 160).

22nd–26th Streets

RAILROAD BARGE AT PIER 66A

Just across the West Side Highway from the Starrett-Lehigh Building is Pier 66A, a historic railway barge that was used to transport boxcars across the Hudson River to the Lackawanna Terminal in New Jersey. The old train tracks, which now cross the Hudson River Greenway's bike path, and a red caboose from the Erie Lackawanna Railroad are still

rich — and once vitally connected — maritime and railroad history.

Today Pier 66A, which sits at the foot of 26th Street (the tall poles visible from the High Line are iron pilings that anchor the huge dock), is home to two venerable work ships that were launched around the same time the High Line opened to locomotives: the *John J. Harvey* fireboat and the *Frying Pan* lightship.

ON THE HIGH LINE

26TH–30TH STREETS

WILDFLOWER FIELD

One of the most beautiful and peaceful landscape settings on the High Line is the Wildflower Field that runs between 27th and 29th Streets. This garden area was planted with a variety of species that were native to the old railroad and grew spontaneously after the trains stopped running. But, like the other gardens, it was designed to be in bloom throughout the growing season, so other plants were introduced and interspersed amongst the natives to ensure a constantly changing blend of colors, styles, and shapes. One highlight is the commingling of two varieties of coneflower, *Echinacea purpurea*: the beautiful purple 'Fatal Attraction' with its white cousin, 'Virgin.' The theatrical *Allium schubertii* with its radiant sphere and bright colors puts on a great show in the late spring and early summer.

The original High Line preservationist [and] charming gadfly who saved the High Line.

— *New York Times,* 2007

It was a terra incognita up there. Unrestricted space. Unimaginable tranquility. It was like looking at the city through a glass bowl.

— Peter Obletz

Of the various characters who have fought over the decades to reclaim the High Line, the most colorful was without doubt Peter Obletz. Obsessed with trains since he was a boy, Obletz paid Conrail ten dollars for the development rights to the High Line in 1984 with a dream to run old parlor cars and locomotives up and down the two-mile stretch for the benefit of tourists, and even to create a light-rail service to Albany. For himself he purchased a 1940s-era Atchison, Topeka and Santa Fe Railway Pullman dormitory — fitted out with bunks for sleeping — and attached it to an old dining car that featured leather seats, stainless-steel walls, and Formica tables. Here, in the shadow of the railroad he loved so much — at just about 30th Street — he would entertain dinner guests on New York Central Railroad china and flatware. His fantasy came undone in a series of political battles with community groups and state officials, and he died at age fifty, having returned the development rights to Conrail. Called by the *New York Times* the "train buff's train buff," Peter Obletz's funeral was held at Grand Central Terminal. Today he is honored, along with others who helped save the High Line, on a plaque in the 14th Street Passage.

Once you lose a rail line, you never get it back,
and who's to say that 20 years later you're
not going to kick yourself from here to Canarsie
that you let it go?

— Peter Obletz

NEW YORK'S LUMBERYARD

During the Industrial Revolution, West Chelsea was a vital hub of New York's manufacturing enterprise, and its riverfront iron works, steam-powered saw mills, stone dressing operations, and acres of lumberyards fed the city's construction boom. There were so many stacks of lumber in the area that a newspaper reporter in 1883 remarked that "the Leaning Tower of Pisa has been copied as nearly as possible in the architecture of these piles." All that's left of the old lumber industry is a small former stable at 554 West 28th Street that was owned by the New York Lumber Auction Company, whose founder, Latimer E. Jones, staged the industry's first auction in the United States, selling lots of oak, Kentucky walnut, ash, "boxwood culls," pine, and other woods.

RADIAL BENCH

The popular block-long radial bench that runs between 29th and 30th Streets recalls the law of nature pronounced by the great urban writer and student of city parks, William "Holly" Whyte: "People tend to sit where there are places to sit." The designers of the High Line took his commandment — *make the place sittable* — to heart, and throughout its extent there is what Whyte would call "an amiable miscellany" of places to perch: benches, stadium and grandstand seats, deck-style lounges, a lawn, French bistro chairs. Like much of the wood throughout the park the long radial bench was made from reclaimed teak.

THE ORIGINAL PEOPLE'S PARK

Before the High Line was transformed into a pastoral urban park, many New Yorkers ventured to cut their way through brambles and shimmy through a broken piece of fence to steal onto the old railroad for a quiet walk. Some of these trespassers on what was the original People's Park have shared photos they took there on the Web: brightly colored graffiti murals painted on rusted corrugated steel fences, exterior walls, stone monuments, and even on the old rail tracks. (One person, becoming meta, scrawled: "Doing graffiti up here is silly.") There are impromptu art installations and sculpture gardens. The photojournalist Ashley Gilbertson waxed nostalgic in the *New York Times* about the wild old elevated railroad, recounting an early visit: "The tracks and sleepers were still in place. The grass and weeds grew higher than my head, and I saw that someone had cleared a plot among them and planted a little vegetable garden. Smashed beer bottles and the occasional crack pipe crunched underfoot. The old covered loading bays that cut into the buildings had become guerrilla art galleries, crammed with graffiti murals by some of New York's legends, and in one case, an illegal iron installation welded to a steel beam."

WILDNESS: PAST, PRESENT, FUTURE

by Rick Darke

The High Line has always been a wild place, but never a wilderness. "Wilderness" is the word we use to conjure a pristine landscape, untouched by humans, where the last best things reside. This

mythic realm is a lovely idea unless you happen to be a human, in which case you're not part of the equation. Humans have always been part of the High Line. In past years when New York Central freight trains plied its tracks, humans took care to control weeds that seeded themselves into the ballast, lest they disrupt the operations of the railroad. But the wildlings outlived the railroad and eventually claimed the landscape, completing their cycles from seed to flower to seed, literally living their lives on the Line. This is the beauty of wildness, in contrast to wilderness. Wildness is regenerative. Wildness is a renewable resource. We humans can play a part in it. We need only to design for a bit less control.

Wildness has been evident on the High Line as long as I've known it, and it still is. Nearly a decade ago, on any given morning, birds scouted the rails and took shelter in the shrubs and grasses, sustained by fruits and seeds. Even a casual visitor could observe the various habitats on display by following a line from the center of the tracks to the shady side of the rail to the coarse gravel

Wildness at the rail yards in May 2005.
Below: Piet Oudolf's layered landscape.

Habitat niches along the line.

holding the sleepers in place. Different plants inhabited different places, their numbers ebbing and flowing with changing conditions. All this is evident along the reconstructed High Line if you look closely. Piet Oudolf's meticulously layered design confidently invites wildness into the equation, celebrating the flux of living populations and the incidental keys to universal processes.

The still-wild rail yards in August 2011, photographed from the Empire State Building.

Early morning birds alight on compass plant as it reclines over the edge of the High Line at 17th Street.

Nature is *"a singular term for the real multiplicity of things and living processes."*

— Raymond Williams
Ideas of Nature, 1980

THE CENTRAL STORES COMPLEX

The Terminal Warehouse and Central Stores complex that takes up the block on West 27th–28th Street between 11th and 12th Avenues is important for architectural and historic reasons. The Central Stores was a pioneer in what would become a long list of storage warehouses in West Chelsea, many of which can still be seen today from the High Line (*pp.152, 182*). The complex, built in the 1880s on land reclaimed from the Hudson River, is enormous, encompassing twenty-four acres and consisting of twenty-five adjoining storage buildings intended to appear as one fortress-like structure: safe and se-cure for anything a person or company might want to leave there. The warehouses stored many things,

from individual household items like furniture, pianos, mirrors, and carpets to merchandise owned by the Wanamaker's and Gimbel Brothers depart-ment stores, prominent in New York at the time. The company also served the many theaters in the area by storing theatrical scenery. There was a separate cold-storage facility for furs, rugs, and woolens; wines, liquors, and rubber were stored in the cellars. The large, arched tunnels were designed to allow trains to pass directly through the complex and across Twelfth Avenue, where boxcars would be floated on company-owned car floats across the Hudson River to New Jersey and then west to the interior of the country. In the 1970s, long after the decline of the railroads, the Terminal Warehouse Building became The Tunnel, a famous nightclub.

THE MAIL TRAINS

The Morgan General Mail Facility, which occupies the full city block between Ninth and Tenth Avenues bounded by 29th and 30th Streets, was completed in 1933 and included a direct connection to the High Line. The outlines of the bricked-up entryway are still visible in the northwest corner where the spur of the viaduct meets the building. As many as 8,000 mail trains a year traveled down the elevated line and crossed Tenth Avenue to enter the second story of the facility. In the 1990s an annex was built between 28th and 29th Streets and connected to the original building by a massive pedestrian bridge. For several years the new structure's huge glazed windows topped the Audubon Society's collision list because so many birds crashed into them and fell to their deaths in the street below. Today the Morgan is one of the largest mail-processing facilities in the nation, handling as many as twelve million pieces of mail in a single day. The giant complex is notable for its combination of old, stately architecture — which includes sculpted eagles carved into a limestone base and friezes depicting floral patterns and geometric shapes — and modern innovation: the new facility had one of the first green roofs in Manhattan, and at 2.5 acres it's one of the largest in the country.

Long before these buildings existed the site was a station owned by the Hudson River Railroad. In February 1861, on the way to his inauguration as president, Abraham Lincoln was the first passenger to use the station. Four years later, on April 25, 1865, his funeral train passed through on its westward journey to Springfield, Illinois.

30TH STREET CUT-OUT

At the northern end of the High Line visitors are invited to peer down through the transparent floor into the bones of the old trestle and see the structural steel beams and girders up close. This is also a fine place for viewing traffic — vehicular and human — as it makes its way along the street below.

HELL'S KITCHEN

The WPA Guide to New York City pronounced Hell's Kitchen "one of the most dangerous areas on the American continent." The neighborhood took its name from the Hell's Kitchen Gang, an 1860s organization of gangsters and hoodlums whose specialty was raids on the New York Central Railroad, which operated many of the trains that ran at street level along Tenth Avenue. To combat the mayhem and robberies the railroad organized a special police force in 1910 and, after much violence that included clubbing and shooting, it finally broke the back of the gangs. The name remained, but today the neighborhood, which begins at 34th Street, is quickly gentrifying.

AMERICA'S OLDEST BED COMPANY

The drab brick building at 517–523 West 29th Street is the former headquarters of the Charles P. Rogers Company, the longest continuously operating manufacturer of beds in the United States. Business took off for the company during the mid-19th century after founder Charles Platt Rogers began fashioning beds from brass and iron, an innovation he pioneered as a way to prevent the bedbugs and vermin that proliferated in wood furniture from creating a home in customers' beds.

In 1955, to celebrate its 100th anniversary, the company sent out invitations for "The Dinner Party of the Century" and invited "Mattress-industry notables . . . to quaff from the Fountain of Youth" at the Biltmore Hotel, one of the many luxury hotels around the country that it supplied with beds. "Are you sleeping too little and aging too fast?" the public relations man asked a reporter for the *New Yorker*. "If so, you will bless the Rogers Rejuvenator Mattress." The company is still a leading supplier of beds and today operates its factory showroom on West 17th Street.

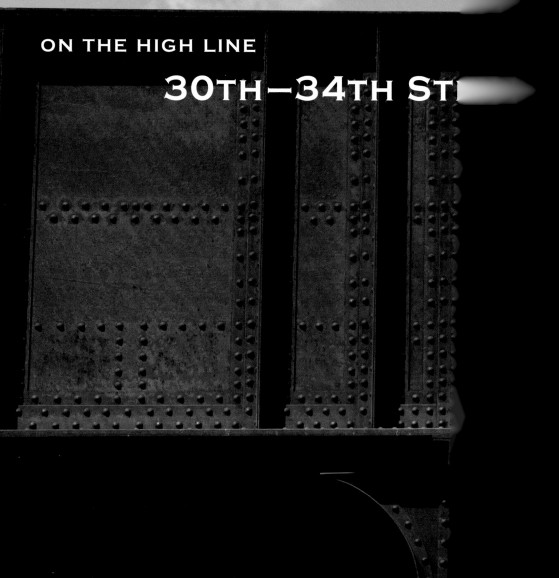

ON THE HIGH LINE

30TH–34TH STR

THE DIVINE WILD CARROT

One of the world's most beautiful weeds is a wonderful patchwork of contradictions. Named for a queen, the plant known to horticulturists as wild carrot is actually just a distant relative of the humble vegetable. No one seems to agree which English queen its popular name refers to — Anne of Denmark, who married King James VI and died in 1619, or Anne of Britain, the last Stuart monarch, who died in 1714. Some point not to a queen but to the patron saint of lace-makers, St. Anne. But whatever the provenance of its name, Queen Anne's lace is a strikingly elegant plant that often — but not always — includes a single dark red flower in its center, perhaps the place where a queen who was an expert lacemaker once pricked her finger and let fall a tiny drop of blood.

It is, for all its delicacy and grace, a sturdy weed that tolerates full sun and dry soil and is commonly found in vacant lots, abandoned grasslands, on stone walls, and along roadsides and railroads. The lacy white clusters known as umbels detach from the plant and come to resemble a bird's nest, another common name for it. The umbels, when they dry out, turn into tumbleweeds, sending the mature plant scatter-ing across the landscape. The seeds of Queen Anne's lace have a particular barbed quality that allows them, after falling into an inhospitable place, to disperse and propagate. This too is a bit of a contradiction since the plant has tradition-ally been used by many cultures as a form of birth control.

At the northern end of the High Line park visitors can peer through the openings of the steel gate and behold a magnificent white carpet of this beautiful plant growing wild, as it has done for so many decades, in the abandoned railbed.

THE HUDSON YARDS

The development of the recently created Hudson Yards district — a total of 360 acres extending west of Eighth Avenue and running between 42nd and 30th Streets, where the High Line currently ends — is one of the largest projects in New York's long history of real estate schemes. The city calls the area "the last frontier" of commercial development in Manhattan. *Times* reporter Joyce Purnick perfectly characterized the average Gothamite's understanding of the plan — which she likened to "a long and often brutal game of three-dimensional monopoly" — when she wrote in 2005: "Nobody ever knows quite what's going on in New York."

When the High Line opened its northern section in 2011, New Yorkers got a new perch from which to view the massive, ongoing project. The heart of the new district, formally known as the John D. Caemmerer West Side Yard, is currently a working rail yard for trains that use Penn Station.

The city rezoned the area and approved a plan to create millions of square feet of commercial and residential projects and open space. It will dramatically change the Hell's Kitchen neighborhood and forever alter the expansive, sun-filled view of the Hudson River and the midtown skyline that can be enjoyed from the northern end of the High Line.

Keep It Wild

When the High Line opened in June 2009 its signature statement, printed on signs nestled in the plantings, was "Keep It Wild." This had been the guiding mandate of the entire preservation project. The wildness of the High Line — the self-seeded plants that grew, over time, into a meadow in the sky — was the spirit of the place that photographer Joel Sternfeld captured and Friends of the High Line dedicated itself to preserving. One segment of the old elevated rail line remains wild: the portion that runs west at 30th Street, with a short jog east toward midtown. When the second half of the park opened in spring 2011 everyone could behold, for the first time, what the early visitors to the former elevated railroad had seen. The grasses still grow wild, and the unkempt quality of the railbed beckons with the whisper of history. We can really imagine trains passing by on those rusty old rails.

In November 2011 one the final episodes in the long, inspiring High Line saga played out in

a series of announcements and press conferences. CSX Transportation had at last agreed to donate the final section of the elevated structure to the city, and the Diller – von Furstenberg Family Foundation pledged $20 million to help complete the project. It was the largest private contribution to a public park in New York City's history. Six months after the second section had opened to triumphant reviews that made the park one of New York's hottest tourist destinations, Friends of the High Line was preparing to launch the final effort of its preservation project. For now, the gate at 30th Street allows a visitor to peer through and see a bit of history while also imagining what the future might bring to this magical park. Much will change in the area, as the Hudson Yards district is developed into a massive new commercial and residential neighborhood. But today, in the middle of Manhattan, we can stand at end of the line and appreciate what that really means: *Keep It Wild*.

Sources and Notes

Every effort has been made to credit sources of information that appear in this book. A quotation from a news source clearly identified in the text with date and publication name — and therefore easily located online — is not cited in *Sources and Notes*, nor are facts about companies, organizations, and buildings that come from an entity's official website. Information about plants was obtained from a combination of books (see *Selected Bibliography*), *TheHighLine.org*, and in consultation with Rick Darke, who has the author's deep gratitude. Errors or omissions are the author's alone. Each note is preceded by the page number on which the reference occurs. Short citations are used for books or articles included in the *Selected Bibliography*. "*NYT*" is an abbreviation for the *New York Times*.

Page

8–11 Valued sources of historical information in the Introduction and throughout the book are the neighborhood reports compiled by the New York City Landmarks Preservation Commission for each district the High Line traverses. See *Selected Bibliography*.

8 "thread that runs through . . . ," Tom Lewis, *The Hudson: A History*, p.5

10 "surrogate Adirondack landscape . . . ," Witold Rybczynski, *A Clearing in the Distance: Frederick Law Olmsted and America in the 19th Century*, New York: Scribner, 1999, p.258

11 "is never the same . . . ," Edwin G. Burrows and Mike Wallace, *Gotham*, p.xxii

41 "Activities begin . . . ," *WPA Guide to New York City*, p.71

43 "a dark melancholy beauty . . . ," Michael Cunningham, "One Street at a Time in Gansevoort Street," *NYT*, 9/16/2001

43 Thirteenth Avenue sources include: *ThirteenthAvenue.blogspot.com*, 8/2/2006; *WilhelmReichTrust.org/trust_history*

43 "very peculiar avenue . . . ," "A Very Peculiar Avenue: A West Side Thoroughfare of Little Account," *NYT*, 11/11/1883

43 "sit on timbers . . . ," "Stroll of a Lounger in a Strange Thoroughfare," *NYT*, 5/9/1886

48 "Its style . . . ," "Ketzel Levine's Talking Plants," National Public Radio, *NPR.org*

54 "a bridge between . . . ," Adam D. Weinberg, "Whitney Museum Sheds Uptown Home for New Meatpacking District Digs," *WNYC.org*

60 DVF Studio: Nico Saieh, "DVF Studio Headquarters / Work AC," *Arch Daily*, 7/15/2008

63 "the north and south facades . . . ," Dana Rubenstein, "'Great Theater' on the High Line," *Wall Street Journal*, 1/31/2011

65 "very high level . . . ," Richard Stalter, "The Flora on the High Line" and private communication with the author

66 "Walking the rails . . . ," from "A World Above: New York Voices," WNET-TV, interview with Rafael Pi Roman, *Thirteen.org*

66 "Please don't let . . . ," from Elizabeth Barlow Rogers, "An Aerial Garden Promenade," *Sitelines*, p.4

68 "tell a story . . . ," from "100 Most Creative People in Business," *Fast Company*

68 "all of my work . . . ," from Sally McGrane, "A Landscape in Winter, Dying Heroically," *NYT*, 1/31/2008

69 "Dying in an interesting way . . . ," from Dan Pearson, "Splendour in the grass," *The Telegraph*, 9/24/2005

69 "a garden isn't . . . ," from Cynthia King, "Garden Guru Piet Oudolf," *Wall Street Journal*, 5/21/2011

74 "in homage to . . . ," High Line Garden Staff, private communication with the author, 6/16/2011

76 Pier Trick: Jan Morris, *Manhattan '45*, Baltimore: The Johns Hopkins University Press, 1986, p.69

80 Felipe Rose, *sallys-hideaway.com/A_History.html*

81 "It was the Wild West . . . ," Irwin Cohen, Dana Rubenstein, "A Market on the Rise," *Wall Street Journal*, 2/13/2011

81 "of a capacity . . . ," Moses King, *King's Handbook of New York City*, p.878

87 French flats: Mary Beth Betts, *Gansevoort Market Historic District Report*, pp.33, 37; Ashby et al., *Interpreting the Views From the High Line*, p.48

87 "It took seven months . . . ," Sam Roberts, "A Discount Mall 11 Stories High Planned in City," *NYT*, 3/12/1984

88 "Oudolf's signature . . . ," Guy Martin, "New York's Hanging Gardens," *Guardian*, 11/7/2009

91 "crammed with graffiti . . . ," Ashley Gilbertson, "Up Over Chelsea, Something Saved, Something Lost," *NYT*, 9/3/2009

94 "rusty trestle's . . . ," Philip Nobel, "High Life on the High Line," *Metropolis*, 5/2002

94 "faithful bay . . . ," "Last 'Cowboy' Rides Over Tenth Ave. Route . . . ," *NYT*, 3/30/41

94 "Far down Tenth Avenue . . . ," Mario Puzo, *The Fortunate Pilgrim*, New York: Ballantine, 1997, p.61

95 "Larry Angeluzzi . . . ," Ibid., p.3

95 "The horses used . . . ," "Cowboys of the Cobblestones," London Terrace *Tatler*, 1/1934

114 "During restoration . . . ," Joshua David and Robert Hammond, *High Line*, p.99

114–15 Sources for Architectural Design Elements include: High Line Garden Staff Tour, May 2011; *Designing the High Line*; *TheHighLine.org/sustainability*

120 "strait-sided . . . ," Christopher Gray, "Are Manhattan's Right Angles Wrong?," *NYT*, 10/23/2005

121 "cartmen, carpenters . . . ," Edwin G. Burrows and Mike Wallace, *Gotham*, p.447

129 "bladder of wind . . . ," Ibid., p.414

131 "The ugliness . . . ," Phillip Lopate, *Waterfront*, p.122

141 Gallery Scene: Kristine Larsen, "Chelsea: It's the New SoHo! Maybe," *New York*, 5/13/1996; "Chelsea: The Metro-Grid Report," *EasternConsolidated.com*, April 2011

147 "big exhibitionist . . . ," "James Corner on Section 2 of the High Line," *Bloomberg.com*

148 "At the core . . . ," John Falk, personal communication with the author

149 "Yes, there might . . . ," Michael Pollan, *Second Nature: A Gardener's Education*, New York: Atlantic Monthly Press, 1991, p.65

151 "thick with spirits . . . ," Cara Buckley, "A Last Night Among the Spirits at the Chelsea Hotel," *NYT*, 7/31/2011

151 Empire Diner: Sam Sifton, "Memories of the Empire Diner," *NYT*, 4/30/2010

152 "rows of closely . . . ," Roger Panetta, *Dutch New York: The Roots of Hudson Valley Culture*, New York: Fordham University Press, 2009, p.96

152 "made her the mistress . . . ," H. M. Williams, "The Warehousing System: Statement of the Condition of the Warehousing Business . . . .," *NYT*, 2/7/1870

152 Manhattan Project: William J. Broad, "Why They Called It the Manhattan Project," *NYT*, 10/30/2007

153 Source for Famous Players: Richard Alleman, *New York: The Movie Lover's Guide*, New York: Broadway Books, 2005, p.231

154 "Hudson River at high tide . . . ," Samuel H. Turner, *Autobiography*, New York: A.D.F. Randolph, 1864, p.123

154 "as early as 1693 . . . ," *Greater New York: Bulletin of the Merchant's Association of New York*, vol. 2, no. 12, 3/24/1913

154 "*New York Times* declared . . . ," "Twenty-One Story Building For Printing Trades, To Be Built . . . ," *NYT*, 1/31/1913

154 "monument of artistic . . . ," *King's Handbook of New York City*, p.896

155 "a kingdom . . . ," *LondonTerraceTowers.com/movieclips*

162 Andrew Jackson Downing quotes: Behula Shah, "The Checkered Career of *Ailanthus altissima*," *Arnoldia*, Harvard University, Fall 1997

162 Cover illustration: Carol Siri Johnson, "Publication of *A Tree Grows in Brooklyn*," New Jersey Institute of Technology, 2003

162 "It would be considered . . . ," Betty Smith, *A Tree Grows in Brooklyn*, New York: Harper Perennial Modern Classics, 2006

164 "something very fine . . . ," Cass Gilbert, "Industrial Architecture in Concrete," *Architectural Forum*, vol. 39, September 1923, pp.84–84, cited in National Register of Historic Places Registration Form

165 Hudson High School: Dana Chivvis, "Homepage High: Teachers, Computers, No Textbooks," *AOLNews.com*, 2/9/2011

165 "its plan . . . ," Amity Shlaes, "Elite Manhattan School Defies Old Preppy Cartel," *Business Week*, 2/28/2011

166 "So atop the city . . . ," *Charles Kuralt's American Moments*, New York: Simon & Schuster, 1999, p.208

169 "eight miles of windows . . . ," Skyscraper Museum, *Skyscraper.org*

175 "aid, care and support . . . ," New York State Constitution, Article XVII

175 "also the site . . . ," Joshua David and Robert Hammond, *High Line: The Inside Story of New York City's Park in the Sky*, p.7

182 "So prevalent . . . ," Phillip Lopate, *Waterfront*, p.142

188–89 Obletz quotes and phrases "original High Line preservationist," "charming gadfly . . . ," all from John Freeman Gill, *NYT*, 5/13/2007

190 "Leaning Tower . . . ," "A Very Peculiar Avenue: A West Side Thoroughfare of Little Account," *NYT*, 11/11/1883; lumber source: "Lumber at Auction," *NYT*, 9/2/1885

190 "People tend to sit . . . ," William H. Whyte, *The Social Life of Small Urban Places*, Washington, D.C.: Conservation Foundation, 1980

192 "The tracks and sleepers . . . ," Ashley Gilbertson, "Up Over Chelsea, Something Saved, Something Lost," *NYT*, 9/3/2009

199 Collision list: James Barron, "Bird Week: The Lure and Danger of the High Line," *NYT*, 5/6/2011

199 Morgan Mail Facility: Alan Feuer, "The Central Nervous System of Mail Delivery," *NYT*, 7/29/2009

201 "Are you sleeping . . . ," "Mattress Dinner," "Talk of the Town," *New Yorker*, 2/12/1955

201 "one of the most dangerous . . . ," *The WPA Guide to New York City*, p.155

205 Divine Wild Carrot sources include Geoffrey Grigson, *The Englishman's Flora;* and Matthew Wood, *The Book of Herbal Wisdom*

206 "last frontier," Hudson Yards Overview, New York City Department of City Planning, *NYC.gov*

Selected Bibliography

Adams, Arthur G. *The Hudson River Guidebook*, 2d ed. New York: Fordham University Press, 1996

Ashby, Reba, et al. *Interpreting the Views From the High Line: Historic Preservation Studio II.* New York: Columbia University Graduate School of Architecture, Planning and Preservation, Spring 2010. *http://arch.columbia.edu/programs/historic-preservation*

Betts, Mary Beth, ed. *Gansevoort Market Historic District Designation Report.* New York City Landmarks Preservation Commission, 2003

Bone, Kevin, ed. *The New York Waterfront: Evolution and Building Culture of the Port and Harbor,* rev. ed. New York: Monacelli Press, 2004

Brazee, Christopher, and Jennifer L. Most. *West Chelsea Historic Designation Report.* New York City Landmarks Preservation Commission, 7/15/2008

Buttenwieser, Ann L. *Manhattan Water-Bound: Manhattan's Waterfront from the Seventeenth Century to the Present.* Syracuse: Syracuse University Press, 1999

Burrows, Edwin G., and Mike Wallace. *Gotham: A History of New York City to 1898.* New York: Oxford University Press, 1999

Carmer, Carl. *The Hudson.* New York: Fordham University Press, 1939

Caro, Robert. *The Power Broker: Robert Moses and the Fall of New York.* New York: Vintage Books, 1974

Chelsea Historic District Designation Report. Landmarks Preservation Commission, 1970

Condit, Carl W. *The Port of New York: A History of the Rail and Terminal System from the Beginnings to Pennsylvania*

Station. Chicago: University of Chicago Press, 1980

Darke, Rick. *The Encyclopedia of Grasses for Livable Landscapes.* Portland: Timber Press, 2007

David, Joshua, and Robert Hammond. *High Line: The Inside Story of New York City's Park in the Sky.* New York: Farrar, Straus and Giroux, 2011

Del Tredici, Peter. *Wild Urban Plants of the Northeast: A Field Guide.* Ithaca: Cornell University Press, 2010

Federal Writers Project. *The WPA Guide to New York City: The Federal Writer's Project Guide to 1930s New York.* New York: New Press, 1939

Friends of the High Line. *Designing the High Line: Gansevoort to 30th Street.* Field Operations, Diller Scofidio + Renfro, Friends of the High Line, The City of New York, 2008

Gerritsen, Henk, and Piet Oudolf. *Dream Plants for the Natural Garden.* Portland: Timber Press, 2000

Grigson, Geoffrey. *The Englishman's Flora.* London: Hard-Davis, MacGibbon, 1975

King, Moses. *King's Handbook of New York City: An Outline History and Description of the American Metropolis.* Boston: Moses King, 1892

Lewis, Tom. *The Hudson: A History.* New Haven: Yale University Press, 2005

Lopate, Phillip. *Waterfront: A Walk Around Manhattan.* New York: Anchor Books, 2004

Mabey, Richard. *Weeds: In Defense of Nature's Most Unloved Plants.* New York: HarperCollins, 2010

New York Central. *West Side Improvement: Initial Stage Dedicated June 28, 1934* (pamphlet)

Rogers, Elizabeth Barlow. "An Aerial Garden Promenade: Nature and Design along the High Line." *Sitelines: A Journal of Place,* vol. 5, no. 2, Spring 2010

Shockley, Jay. *Greenwich Village Historic District Extension Designation Report.* New York City Landmarks Preservation Commission, 2006

Stalter, Richard. "The Flora on the High Line, New York City, NY." *Journal of the Torrey Botanical Society,* vol. 131, no. 4, October–December 2004, pp.387–93

Special Hudson Yards District Zoning Resolution. Article X: Special Purpose Districts, Chapter 3: Special Hudson Yards District. The City of New York, 02/02/2011

West Chelsea Special District, Establishment of Special West Chelsea District. Article IX, Chapter 8: The Special West Chelsea District. The City of New York, 6/23/2005

White, Norval, Elliot Willensky, and Fran Leadon. *AIA Guide to New York City,* 5th ed. Oxford University Press, 2010

Wildflower.org. The University of Texas at Austin, Lady Bird Johnson Wildflower Center

Wyman, Donald. *Wyman's Gardening Encyclopedia,* 6th ed. New York: Scribner, 1977

Wood, Matthew. *The Book of Herbal Wisdom: Using Plants as Medicine.* Berkeley: North Atlantic Books, 1997

ACKNOWLEDGMENTS

A small team of people put this book together, including Lorraine Ferguson, art director and designer, and Thomas Dyja, editor and guiding hand for the entire project. We were exceedingly lucky to have contributions from author, photographer, and landscape ethicist Rick Darke. Rick has been photographing the High Line since 2002, long before it became the place it is today, and has deep knowledge about its history and preservation. Beyond being a teacher to us all he was a joy to work with. Our richly talented photographers, Scott Mlyn and Juan Valentin, spent countless days and nights in the park in quest of the right shot. Rick, Scott, and Juan all saw and captured things on the High Line that we would have otherwise missed, and their contributions cannot be overstated. We are also grateful to Scott for providing valuable picture editing expertise along the way to the finished book. We thank Marty Schnure for her excellent work on the map as well as her endless patience and good cheer as we tweaked and refined it.

The three of us wish to thank the following people for the help and support they provided during the course of writing, researching, and designing *On The High Line*: Robert Adams, Vincent Ashbahian, John Baeder, Andre Balazs, Mike Barnett, Kim Beck, Catherine Belloy, Heather Darcy Bhandari, Flora Biddle, Tanya Blum, Rustie Brook and the Municipal Arts Society, Caroline Burghardt, David Byrne, Peter Davidson, Peter Del Tredici, Kyla Dippong, Anita Duquette, Jeffrey Eaton, Mike Epstein, John Falk, Thomas Flagg, Andrea Glimcher, Suzanne Gluck, Robert Gober, Ann Godoff, Sarah Goulet, Dan Graham, Federico Grandicelli, Keith Gray, Tim Griffin, Arjun Gupta, Matthew Higgs, Joey Jalleo, James Jenkins, Janet Jenkins, John Jobaggy, Mary Habstritt, Sam Hammer, Sarah Kovach, Suzanne Kreps, Albert LaFarge, Pier LaFarge, Diane Laska-Swanke, Heather and Ralph Lee, Molly Lehnhardt, Carol, Sophia and Eva LeWitt, Matthew Lyons, Jack MacRae, Daniela Maerky, Fernanda Meza, Margaret Morton, Justin Neal, Brooke Garber Neidich, Daniel Neidich, Graham Newhall, Douglas L.

Obletz, Piet Oudolf, Adriana Pellegrini, Jeffrey Peabody, Laura Raicovich, Mark Reiter, Peter Richards, Tony Robins, LeeAnn Rossi, Rick and Monica Segal, Amie Scally, Kerry Scheidt, Davina Semo, David Sharps, Talia Shulze, Deirdre and Gary Smerillo, Tammy Smith, Stephen Soba, Katie Sonnenborn, Richard Stalter, Sarah Sze, Lumi Tan, Adam D. Weinberg, Wilbur Woods. Special thanks to Joel Sternfeld for generously allowing us to reproduce a selection of his photographs of the wild High Line.

We have worked in and around the book business for many years, and throughout the course of working on this project not a day went by when we didn't appreciate how lucky we are to have Will Balliett as our publisher. At Thames & Hudson we also thank Susan Dwyer, Elizabeth Keene, and Tiffany Alvorado McKenna, and at W. W. Norton, Debra Morton Hoyt.

Our team has no formal affiliation with Friends of the High Line, the group that saved and maintains the park, but this book would not, of course, exist without the vision and dogged determination of Joshua David and Robert Hammond, its founders. At Friends of the High Line we particularly thank Kate Lindquist for her comments and corrections to the manuscript. The High Line is supported by private and corporate donations and by the City of New York. To become a member or to make a donation, visit *TheHighLine.org*.

INDEX

PHOTOGRAPHY CREDITS

Copyright for each image is retained by the photographer.

Adelaide Balliett
Page 125 *middle*.

Rick Darke
Front UK cover *top, bottom left*.
Back UK cover.
Back US cover *top left, top right, bottom*.
Front US cover flap *top left*.
Back US cover flap *bottom left*.
Inside front flap *top right*.
Inside back flap *middle*.
Pages 12–13; 14 *top right, bottom*; 15 *top left, top right, middle*; 16–23; 25–29; 44 *bottom*; 48 *bottom right*; 49; 64–65; 68–69; 80 *top*; 82 *bottom*; 86 *bottom*; 88 *top, middle right*; 89 *top*; 106–07; 114 *bottom right*; 115 *top left, bottom*; 116–119; 128; 129 *top, second from top, third from top*; 138 *top, bottom right*; 139 *top*; 156–57; 174; 192–97; 204–211.

Kaye Dyja
Page 215.

Thomas Dyja
Pages 83 *top*; 109 *top right, bottom left*.

Mike Epstein
Pages 138 *bottom left*; 139 *middle left, bottom left, bottom right*.

Friends of the High Line
Page 129 *bottom*.

Annik La Farge
Front UK cover *middle right*.
Front US cover *middle*.
Pages 44 *top*; 48 *top*; 78 *top left*; 88 *middle left*; 99 *bottom*; 103 *middle, bottom left*; 104 *bottom right*; 105 *bottom right*; 120–21; 130 *top, bottom left*; 135; 145 *bottom*; 155; 160–61; 166; 167 *top left, top right, bottom middle, bottom right*; 172; 173 *top*; 175 *bottom*; 199 *bottom*.

Scott Mlyn
Front UK cover *middle left*.
Front US cover *top, bottom left, bottom right*.
Back US cover *middle*.
Front US cover flap *top right, bottom*.
Back US cover flap *top left, top right, middle, bottom right*.
Inside front flap *bottom left, bottom right*.
Inside front cover.
Inside back cover.
Inside back flap *top right, bottom left, bottom right*.
Pages 1–7; 11; 36–38; 39 *top right, bottom*; 42; 45–47; 48 *bottom left*; 60; 63 *bottom*; 70; 71 *bottom*; 72–73; 74 *middle, bottom*; 77 *top*; 78 *top right*; 79 *top*; 81; 84–85; 87 *top*; 88 *bottom*; 91–93; 96–97; 100–101; 103 *top, bottom right*; 110 *top*; 112 *top, bottom right*; 114 *top left, bottom left*; 120 *left*; 122–23; 127 *bottom*; 132–33; 134 *bottom*; 136–37; 141 *bottom*; 144 *top*; 146; 148–49; 158–59; 163; 167 *bottom left*; 168 *top, bottom right*; 169 *top left, bottom right*; 171; 176–77; 180–81; 183–85; 200; 202–03.

Juan Valentin
Inside front flap *top left, middle*.
Inside back flap *top left*.
Pages 39 *top left*; 40; 41 *top left, top right, bottom*; 43; 50–53; 56 *top*; 57; 58 *bottom*; 59; 61–62; 63 *top*; 71 *middle*; 74 *top*; 75; 76; 77 *middle, bottom*; 78 *bottom*; 79 *bottom*; 80 *bottom*; 82 *top*; 83 *middle, bottom left, bottom right*; 87 *bottom*; 89 *top*; 90; 98; 99 *top*; 102; 104 *top, bottom left*; 105 *top*; 108; 109 *top left, middle, bottom right*; 110 *bottom*; 112 *bottom left*; 114 *top right*; 115 *top right*; 124; 125 *top, bottom*; 126; 127 *top*; 130 *bottom right*; 131; 134 *top left*; 145 *top*; 147; 150; 152; 154; 164–65; 168 *bottom left*; 169 *top right, middle, bottom right*; 170 *left*; 173 *middle*; 175 *top*; 179; 186–87; 198; 190–91; 198; 199 *top*; 201.

Joey Weiman
Page 56 *bottom*.

ON THE HIGH LINE

Thomas Dyja
Concept and editor

Lorraine Ferguson
Art director and design

Marty Schnure
Cartography

Barbara Gogan
Copy editor

Janet Jenkins
Proofreader

Principal Photographers

Rick Darke
is a widely published author, photographer, lecturer, and consultant focused on contextual landscape design and management. His books include *The American Woodland Garden, The Encyclopedia of Grasses for Livable Landscapes,* and *The Wild Garden: Expanded Edition.* Visit *rickdarke.com*

Scott Mlyn
is a photographer, magazine picture editor, author, consultant, and director of videos using still pictures. His photographs have appeared in books and magazines, and he is the author of *Before the Game*, a photography book on Major League Baseball. Visit *scottmlyn.com*

Juan Valentin
hails from the town of San Sebastian in Puerto Rico. He currently works as a counselor for the New York City Department of Education and resides in Chelsea.

Copyright
© 2012 Ferla Fardy, LLC

First published in 2012 in paperback in the United States of America by Thames & Hudson Inc. 500 Fifth Avenue New York, New York 10110 *thamesandhudsonusa.com*

Published in the United Kingdom in 2012 by Thames & Hudson Ltd. 181A High Holborn London WC1V 7QX *thamesandhudson.com*

Library of Congress Catalogue Card Number 2011934551

ISBN 978-0-500-29020-0

British Library Cataloguing-in-Publication Data A catalogue record for this book is available from the British Library

Printed in China by Oceanic Graphic International, Inc.

Future Editions
The High Line park currently occupies just over two-thirds of the old railroad viaduct. The final section, from 30th–34th Streets, has not yet been completed. To be alerted when a new edition of **ON THE HIGH LINE** is available, please join the mailing list at *HighLineBook.com*